Mike Gonzalez, a historian and literary critic, is Emeritus Professor of Latin American Studies at the University of Glasgow. He writes extensively on Latin America and is the author of *The Gathering of Voices: The Twentieth-Century Poetry of Latin America*; *Che Guevara and the Cuban Revolution*; *Tango: Sex and Rhythm of the City*; and *A Rebel's Guide to Marx*.

'Mike Gonzalez's fluently written, stimulating guide to Barcelona's literature covers dozens of books in Catalan, Castilian Spanish and English. It is, too, much more than a literary guide, as its author finds in the writing from and about the city a way into explaining its history, politics and social life.'

Michael Eaude,
author of *Barcelona: The City that Reinvented Itself*

'I've waited years for a book like this to appear! A passionate, comprehensive and sensitive study, the author reveals an intimate knowledge of Barcelona's urban rhythms, history and culture, all of which come alive throughout its pages – essential reading for anyone with an interest in the subject.'

Chris Ealham,
author of *Anarchism and the City: Revolution and Counter-Revolution in Barcelona, 1898–1937*

Barcelona

A LITERARY GUIDE FOR TRAVELLERS

Mike Gonzalez

I.B. TAURIS
LONDON · NEW YORK

Copyright © 2019 Mike Gonzalez

The right of Mike Gonzalez to be identified as the author of this work has been asserted by the author in accordance with the Copyright, Designs and Patents Act 1988.

Every attempt has been made to gain permission for the use of the images in this book. Any omissions will be rectified in future editions.

References to websites were correct at the time of writing.

ISBN: 978 1 78831 122 9
eISBN: 978 1 78672 475 5
ePDF: 978 1 78673 475 4

A full CIP record for this book is available from the British Library
A full CIP record is available from the Library of Congress

Library of Congress Catalog Card Number: available

Typeset by JCS Publishing Services Ltd
Printed and bound in Great Britain

CONTENTS

Illustrations

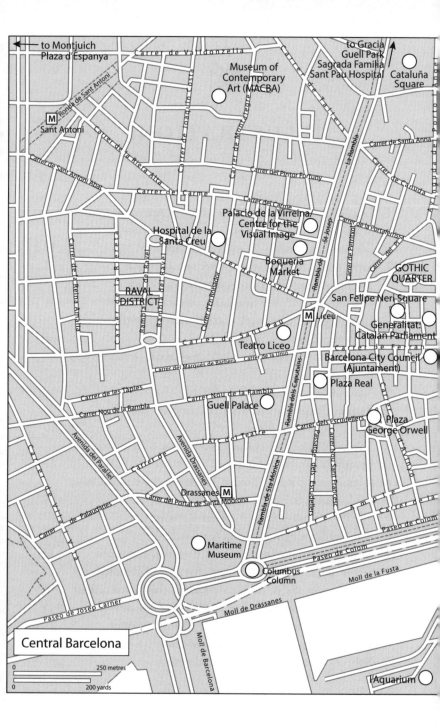

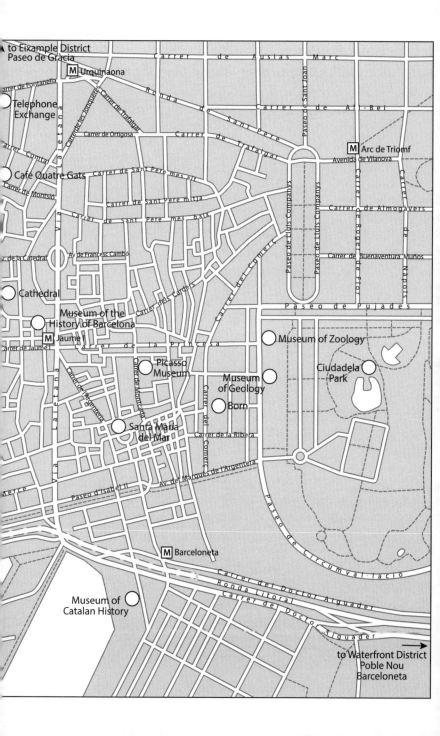

Acknowledgements

The opportunity to write this guide has allowed me to honour a debt to my father. Antonio González Cruz was born in the Raval, in the Carrer Hospital – the very heart of radical Barcelona. He was a member of the Communist Party, and one of the tens of thousands who were forced to leave Spain when fascism destroyed the Republic. He found his way, eventually, to Britain. His exile lasted until 1978. In the year when he returned to his beloved city, I came to meet him – and discovered how deeply Catalan he was – and that throughout his 40 years of exclusion he had continued to write and speak his own language as well as Castilian.

And for Dominic, Rachel and Anna and my beautiful grandchildren – this glimpse of the world your grandfather/great-grandfather came from.

To Marianella and Martha Lucia, who shared my explorations and the ups and downs of writing. I hope this book will bring us even closer to the world we have entered together.

Andy Durgan, a committed and insightful historian of the Spanish Civil War and of Barcelona, and a cherished friend, reintroduced me to the city he has lived in for three decades, and which he loves. Without him, I would have missed or misread many things. His partner Isa added to and enriched his insights and gave generously of her friendship, for which I am deeply grateful.

My thanks to Mike Eaude for his fine writing on Barcelona, Cataluña and on the work of Vázquez Montalbán.

Helena Cobos is the dedicated librarian of Altafulla, the town where I live. Without her passion for the literature of Cataluña, and her wonderful local library, this guide would have been impossible.

To Rosa Maria, for her willingness to share her knowledge and experience with these strange new neighbours.

1

A SLOW STROLL DOWN
THE RAMBLAS

On 12 December 1935, Federico García Lorca's newest play, and his last, *Doña Rosita the Spinster* opened at the Teatro Principal, off Barcelona's iconic avenue, the Ramblas. The leading role was played by Margarita Xirgu, the greatest actor of her time. Lorca himself (he was an accomplished musician) provided the piano accompaniment. It was a huge success. A few days later, the flower-sellers of the Ramblas, who had provided the quantities of roses bought by an adoring public, were invited to a special performance – the first time, he said, that flower-sellers had come to meet a poet. It is recalled in Miguel Garcia-Posada's introduction to Lorca's *Complete Works* (1996):

> Tonight (he said), my youngest and dearest child, Doña Rosita, has worked for the charming flower sellers of the Rambla, with their open smiles and their moist hands. It is my privilege to dedicate this performance to them [. . .] The one street on earth I hope will never end, where the four seasons of the year coexist, with its rich sounds, its breezes, its ancient blood, is Barcelona's Rambla.
>
> They say, and it is true, that no Barcelonan can sleep easy in his bed unless he has strolled along the Rambla, and I have felt the same in the days I have spent in this beautiful city. The essence of Barcelona, the eternal, the incorruptible, the great, is here on this street. On one side the Gothic district, where you can hear the sound of fountains and the strumming of a fifteenth-century

lute. On the other, crowded, cruel, incredible, you will hear the accordions of the world's sailors, the flutter of painted lips and the raucous dawn laughter.

It was to be Lorca's last visit to the city he had visited many times with Salvador Dalí, the painter. Less than a year later, at the beginning of the Spanish Civil War, he was murdered in retaliation for his support for the Republic. But others followed him, as so many had come before, in search of the medieval city or the forbidden pleasures of the Raval, the Chinese Quarter. Literally millions have taken that walk along the wide boulevard, slowed by the bewildering density of the crowds, past the flower stalls and the caged birds and animals, pausing from time to time to gape quizzically at the living statues or pointing ahead to Christopher Columbus gazing out over the port where the avenue ends.

The Ramblas (there are five: Rambla de Canaletes, Rambla de los Estudios, Rambla de las Flores, Rambla de Capuchinos and Rambla de Santa Monica) are the main artery of the city, a walkway between two of Barcelona's several worlds, witness to its changes, its contradictions, its expansions and its tragedies – the latest a terrible and mindless terrorist attack on the slow-moving crowds in 2017.

The Ramblas capture much of the history of Barcelona: the eighteenth-century palaces of the newly wealthy or the eternally rich, the Modernista shops with their beautiful elaborate façades, the Boquería market groaning with plenty, the Liceu theatre repeatedly re-emerging from its own ashes, the International Hotel that welcomed Einstein, Hemingway and Buffalo Bill among others in its 100-year-long history, the thirteenth-century Santa Creu hospital that gave refuge to the poor and the destitute in the Middle Ages. Most of these buildings have survived the city's changes, though some now house the tourist traps that advertise their wares by hanging Barça shirts bearing the names of Messi or Neymar along the pavements. To one side the Raval is still a refuge for those who travel to the city in search of work and hope, as well as offering a promise of the forbidden. To the other, the Gothic Quarter, the Barri Gòtic, whose false Gothic façades and genuine Roman wall and medieval palaces still hold their mystery.

Writers, painters, travellers, wanderers, pickpockets, fortune-tellers, searchers after truth and others looking for more immediate sensations have, over the centuries, walked the length of the Ramblas, between Cataluña Square and the Columbus statue. The Gothic Quarter, the medieval city enclosed within walls until they were demolished in the mid-nineteenth century, is a labyrinth of dark narrow streets, where washing still hangs from balconies as it must have done since time immemorial. Even in the modern city it is eerily quiet in the evening, until you turn a corner into an unexpected square where it is conversation that you hear.

George Sand arrived in Barcelona in 1838 with her lover, the composer Frederic Chopin, on their way to Mallorca, where they hoped the clean sea air would ease Chopin's tuberculosis. Travelling through Cataluña, a journey she recounted in *A Winter in Mallorca* (1842), they encountered bandits and guerrillas and a general state of war, until they reached Barcelona:

We crossed the immense, formidable fortifications of Barcelona. I lost count of the gates, the drawbridges, the posterns and the Rampart; all announced that we were entering a city at war. Behind a triple line of cannons, and isolated from the rest of Spain by banditry and civil strife, the bright youth strolled in the sun along the Rambla, a long avenue lined by trees and buildings, like our boulevards. The women are beautiful, graceful and coquettish, concerned only with the folds of their mantillas and the games their suitors play; the men occupied with their cigars, laughing, chattering, watching the ladies, discussing Italian opera, and apparently unconcerned with what was happening beyond the walls. But when night fell, the opera ended and the guitars stopped playing, the city was delivered to the hands of the watchmen; everything fell silent amid the monotonous sound of the sea, except for the strident cries of the sentinels, and the sounds of shots at irregular intervals, now occasional, now in volleys, sometimes far away, sometimes close by, until the early morning. Then everything was quiet again for an hour or two, and the bourgeoisie seemed to be sleeping deeply, while the port awoke and the sailors began their activity.

If during the hours of the promenade and pleasure you asked what were those strange frightening noises during the night, the reply, delivered with a smile, was that that was nobody's business and it wasn't wise to ask.

Ruben Darío, the Nicaraguan poet and Latin America's leading Modernista, visiting the city for the first time in 1899, described the Ramblas in a report for the Buenos Aires newspaper *La Nación*; he was struck by the social mix of the crowds:

Along this avenue, coming and going, the bowler hat and the workman's cap, the dinner jacket and the open shirt, the fine lady and the whore rub shoulders. Past the lines of trees where a million sparrows chirp and chatter, the human river flows by the stalls selling flowers, grapes, oranges, birds and fresh dates from Africa.

The Ramblas were once a stream flowing down from the Collserola where Tibidabo now sits. It ran past the city walls and carried most of its waste and detritus to the waters of the port. Clustered around the city gates and along the wall, the city's marginal population, its undesirables, lived and worked. There were Gypsies, migrants, prostitutes and thieves, as well as the trades that were regarded by the citizens as unhealthy or corrupt. The streets outside the walls carried their names – the butchers, the purveyors of goat's meat, the ropemakers (presumably because of their association with the scaffold). Beyond the Ramblas were the small farms that fed the city, and the religious institutions – convents and monasteries –

that occupied large tracts of the hinterland. The snaking paths that led along its banks began to be replaced by straight roads in the mid-eighteenth century, giving access to the open land that would become the Raval.

The grand avenue of the old town was Montcada Street, where the wealthiest nobility had their mansions, well away from the crowded streets at its centre. Two of those grand houses are occupied today by the Picasso Museum. They belonged to the old landed aristocracy, whose ancestral estates provided their income. But by the eighteenth century there was a new emerging layer of wealth. The *indianos*, as they were called, were those who had made their fortunes across the Atlantic in the Americas.

The original restrictions on trade with Spanish America excluded the Catalans. Their dominion was the Mediterranean, but what for a couple of centuries had been their domination of that trade began to diminish as rivals and competitors from Italy and Turkey, among others, reduced the scale of their operations.

The siege of the city in 1714, whose anniversary on 11 September (La Diada) is commemorated by vast concentrations of Catalans, devastated much of the old town. In the decades that followed, and despite the continued rural resistance to domination from Madrid, Catalan agricultural production improved and fed the population of the growing city. In Barcelona, industries were emerging, especially textiles, owned by the landed families of the interior. But it was an unintended consequence of the imposition of rule from Madrid that fuelled Cataluña's economic growth. The Spanish markets, and the consumers in the Spanish colonies, now became accessible to the Catalans and their luxury exports: cottons, silks, the ceramics for which Cataluña was famous and the crude cognac which was favoured in the Americas. The first Catalan ship, *Nuestra Senyora de Montserrat* sailed in 1745, and the sugar, coffee and chocolate from the Caribbean that the maritime traffic brought back became hugely popular among the urban middle classes. By 1778 the ban on Catalan involvement in the Atlantic trade was finally lifted.

Textiles were the Catalan speciality, particularly the decorated cotton textiles called *indianas*. They were much sought after in the Americas. The first factory producing these printed cotton fabrics was opened in Barcelona in 1737. Its machinery was still fairly primitive, but the Catalan countryside provided plentiful cheap labour – and the culture of imperial Spain still looked askance at the business of manufacture, which meant that Barcelona faced no internal competition. At that time it was still a mainly domestic or small-scale industry, but it was changing with the times and with mechanisation.

In 1767 the newly formed Manufacturers' Association, the Junt de Comerç, enforced a regulation that cotton cloth could only be produced in factories containing a minimum of 12 looms. This was almost certainly a response to the new technology of cotton production arriving from England, like the spinning jenny and the water frame. Though it was still well behind industrial developments in England, Cataluña was at the leading edge in the Spanish state. The ban on cotton production in France, designed to protect its silk weaving industry, added to Cataluña's competitive advantage at this critical moment of growth, though it also ensured the disappearance of the small-scale, often domestic production which had survived until then. Thenceforward, the once independent weavers would work for the factory owners.

This was a triangular trade. Catalan ships sailed to the coast of Africa to collect slaves, whom they then transported to the Caribbean – particularly to Cuba. From the Antilles came the sugar, and the coffee and chocolate, that found such a ready market in Barcelona. More importantly, Catalan ships sailed on to North America and loaded cotton from the American South. This transatlantic trade benefited both old landowning families and new merchants.

New buildings close to the port marked this prosperity. The Llotja, the stock exchange, and the Aduana, the customs building, joined the earlier generations of monumental buildings – the fourteenth-century Consulado del Mar (Consulate of the Seas) and the Drassanes, the shipyard built in the same period, which now houses the Maritime Museum.

The Ramblas, too, would enter a new phase of their life later in the eighteenth century. In 1776, under the Conde de Asalto, the rebuilding of the Ramblas began, widening the avenue and enclosing the Cagalella River beneath. The Count also built the first streets into what is now the Raval, the first of which bears his name. The vast fortunes earned by some in the American trade, the *indianos,* financed the early industrial development of the city – but there was plenty left over to build great houses along and around the Ramblas. The Casa March de Reus and the Palau Mojá overlooked the new avenue. The first to be built, in 1776, belonged to the notorious Manuel de Amat i Junyent.

Amat came from an aristocratic Catalan family but entered the service of the Spanish Crown, first as a soldier and later as viceroy, the king's representative, in Chile and Peru. The authority of the viceroy was enormous and for many, like Amat, provided unimaginable opportunities for self-enrichment – especially since with the post came control of the rich silver mines of Potosí, in what is now Bolivia, on behalf of the Spanish Crown. Considerable effort has gone into representing Amat as a loyal and honest public servant, but that is a little difficult to reconcile with the plans he sent to Barcelona for his new residence and the huge expense involved in furnishing and decorating it. Named the Palacio de la Virreina – for his wife, the *virreina* – it is now the Centre for the Visual Image, staging frequent and informative exhibitions about the city.

By the time he arrived in Barcelona, Amat was already over 70; he had left Peru under a cloud because of the behaviour of his lover Micaela Villegas, known as La Pericholi (a pet name that was in fact a mispronunciation of a far less flattering epithet coined by the outraged Viceroy). She was a well-known and scandalous figure in the Peruvian theatre, though it was her open and public relationship with Amat, by whom she bore a son, that provoked the most persistent gossip. It was her assault on her fellow actor and producer with a whip that led to her disgrace and ultimately to Amat's departure. Her reputation, and her ability to ride public opinion, turned her into something of a heroine – Offenbach's operetta *La Perichole* was inspired by Prosper Merimée's novel about her (he also wrote *Carmen*), and she reappears in the American writer Thornton Wilder's novel and play *The Bridge of San Luis Rey* (1927) as the lover of Uncle Pío, an adventurer and teacher.

When Amat returned to Barcelona, Micaela stayed behind, well-provided for by her elderly lover; she lived a less scandalous life thereafter. Amat, on the other hand, married his niece, almost 50 years his junior, and continued the life of a libertine for his few remaining years. Although his original designs were far too grand for his building plot, his palace remained the largest on the avenue. After his death, his widow lived on there in some luxury, much to the disapproval of Catalan society, scandalised that a widow on her own should occupy these vast, luxurious apartments. During the Spanish Civil War the building was taken over by the Partido Obrero de Unificación Marxista (POUM, the Workers' Party of Marxist Unification), the revolutionary socialist organisation led by Andreu Nin.

Just beyond it is the Santa Creu hospital, which took in the waifs and strays of the medieval city. Its interior is an unexpectedly quiet place, despite the busy surroundings. Two streets further down is the Guell Palace designed by Gaudí for his mentor Eusebi Guell. The Guell family were among the wealthiest of the *indianos*. Their fortune was invested by Eusebi's father in the first factory for textile machinery, La Máquina Terrestre, which opened in the 1830s. Eusebi eventually married the heiress to the greatest of the *indiano* fortunes, the daughter of Antonio López y López, the Marquis of Comillas, banker, and owner of Barcelona's Transatlantic Shipping Company.

The Teatro Principal, where Lorca's plays were staged, opposite the Santa Creu hospital, was the city's first theatre, but the Teatro Liceu, on the Ramblas, was its most iconic. It was built in 1844 and opened three years later. As Michael Eaude puts it in *Barcelona: The City that Reinvented Itself* (2008):

> Opera was of course the nineteenth century bourgeois art form par excellence, so it is entirely appropriate that Barcelona, the Manchester of Spain, should have had a luxurious, internationally renowned opera house, second in size only to La Scala Milan, whereas Madrid, with no real middle class in the nineteenth century except state bureaucrats, could never sustain one. As well as being a symbol of Catalan wealth, inevitably the Liceu was an object of envy from the state capital. Nothing pleased the Catalan industrialists more as they discussed business over their lobsters and cava in the sumptuous private rooms of the Liceu. For it was not just a theatre, it was a private club for conducting business with pleasure.

But it was a bomb that launched the theatre into the city's consciousness most dramatically. The Liceu was a place to see and be seen, but opera was also popular with the lower classes, and the fifth-level gallery catered to a working-class public – with a separate entrance, of course. In the 1890s, the bourgeois opera-going public favoured the Italian style, and the 1893 season opened on 7 November that year with Rossini's *William Tell*. At the beginning of the second act, Santiago Salvador, an anarchist, launched two Orsini bombs from the upper gallery into the stalls where the rich sat. Twenty people were killed, though the second bomb did not explode (it is now displayed in the Museum of the History of Barcelona).

In his novel *Mariona Rebull* (1947), Ignacio Agustí describes the aftermath of the bomb. Mariona, a romantic young woman from an old rural Catalan family, is married to Joaquín Rius, who runs the family textile factory in the Raval district. His family, unlike Mariona's, do not come from old money; they belong to a new class of successful entrepreneurs in the modern Barcelona economy. Joaquín is entirely devoted to the business of making money; he is calculating and cold, and his marriage – despite his early declarations of love – serves his social ambitions. He neglects Mariona, who is then seduced by a schoolfriend of Joaquín's whose aristocratic background and culture creates a sharp contrast with the pragmatic Joaquín. Mariona has gone to the opera to meet her lover. Rius is in the factory when the news of the bomb reaches him. He rushes to the theatre:

> The theatre was a mass of twisted seats, wood, glass, and torn velvet. And above and between the gaps bodies were piled, their faces unrecognisable. There were silks soaked with blood whose smell rose in the air. The crowd pushed and strained in the doorways, unable to move and hating one another, frightened and crowded together.
>
> Joaquín withdrew into the box. He had to hold the curtain to stay upright. A terrible vertigo had taken hold. He had to assuage the emptiness in his heart, control the breathing that had taken control of him; he had to do something, something useful, find his wife, pick her up and carry her home. Mariona wouldn't be able to bear this, without him. God help me to find her! But then he saw the open fan of the widow Torra, her white hand gently holding it still. She hadn't even been able to close her fan! And peering over the balcony he saw the lady's fixed smile, unmoving, placid. He would have liked to close her eyes, those eyes empty of expression. But he had to find Mariona.

In fact both Mariona and her lover are among the dead.

Salvador belonged to the anarchist current that favoured direct action. His bomb was in retaliation for the execution of Paulino Pallas, executed a month earlier for the attempted assassination of the Captain General of Cataluña, Martínez Campos.

In 1896, another bomb aimed at the Corpus procession (the subject of a famous painting by Ramon Casas) claimed three more deaths, though it seems that it was the work of an agent provocateur.

In 1897, the murder of Prime Minister Cánovas by Angiolillo would in turn avenge the executed Salvador.

In nineteenth-century Barcelona, the Ramblas were still a space where the wealthy promenaded, though, as Ruben Darío observed, they had to rub shoulders there with the inhabitants of the Raval. The avenue would often become a space of conflict too, when the social encounter became a confrontation. Then, as now, it was the scene of processions and rituals, but also of protests and clashes between elements of the population and the forces of order, as we shall see.

The year 1835 was highly significant in the life of the Ramblas. At first sight, the burning of churches and religious institutions may seem to be little more than vandalism. The widespread fires lit across Barcelona in the summer of 1835 would seem to belong to that class of wanton destruction, particularly since the explanation often given is that it all began with a *corrida*, a bullfight organised on 26 July in the wooden bullring near the Ciutadella, to celebrate the Queen's birthday. It was apparently not outstanding, and an irate crowd, displeased with the performance of bulls and *toreros* alike, began to throw seat cushions into the arena. So far, so normal. Others in the crowd, however, found a rope and tied it around the horns of one of the animals, leading it towards the Ramblas. Robert Hughes, in his *Barcelona* (2001), quotes a popular ballad explaining that:

> On the night of St James
> In 1835,
> There was a fight
> Inside the bullring.
> Three bulls came out
> They were all pretty bad
> And that was why the people
> Set fire to the convents.

The anonymous balladeer was only partly right. In fact the first burnings were in the city of Reus, near Tarragona, in response to the murder of some liberals by local Carlists.

Cataluña at the time was the scene of a continuing and bitter guerrilla war between the supporters of Don Carlos, the son of the deeply conservative King Ferdinand VII, and the Catalans. The King, who died in 1833, nominated his three-year-old daughter Isabel as his successor instead. The Carlists, as the supporters of Don Carlos were called, then launched a war in the Catalan countryside. Carlos was deeply disliked by liberals for his extreme reactionary views. His claim became the focus of discontent for Catholic conservatives, for whom the abolition of the rights of the Inquisition represented a wider penetration of liberal, anti-clerical ideas, and a cause for all the more reactionary forces hostile to liberalism. Their agitation would continue for over 30 years in a continual guerrilla war in inland Cataluña, though its most damaging and destructive phase lasted through most of the 1830s.

The Carlists reserved particular rage for anything that smacked of industry and, by extension, of the city. Any small factory outside urban boundaries would be burned to the ground or destroyed; ironically, many of the dispossessed peasantry who were the victims of their scorched-earth policies then made their way to the burgeoning industries of the city. Fire, as an instrument of revenge or an expression of class hatred, would launch the next phase of Barcelona's growth.

Barcelona was a resolutely liberal city, while inland, rural Cataluña was the scene of violent confrontations. It is possible that a proportion of the crowd on 26 July 1835 were recent immigrants from the countryside who had fled the rural violence. The persistent rumour that the Carlists, who were closing in on Barcelona, intended to use the bullfight as an opportunity for an attack or even for a coup, would have resonated with the public. The spark that set the whole thing ablaze might well have been the poor quality of the performance of both animals and men. But the causes of the riot, if we can call it that, and of the series of church burnings that followed, lie in the deeper reality, though the fire-raisers were certainly encouraged by the agitation of the liberal orators exploiting the opportunity to attack the Carlists. Anger and frustration at the material conditions of Barcelona at the time would have been a common currency, particularly among the poor living in the dark and insanitary conditions of the Barri Gòtic and the Raval. At one level, the riot served to avenge a hundred grievances, and for once to allow the poor to emerge from their dark basements into the street.

Whatever the case, the Church and its advocates were the enemy of liberal Barcelona, and the crowds went on a rampage through the city. The twelfth-century Cistercian abbey at Poblet, sacked by local peasants, and the Benedictine monastery at Sant Cugat were early victims, while in the heart of the city the church and convent of El Carme, an important thirteenth-century building, were razed to the ground. It was a complex protest, against a reactionary Church which was continuing to wreak havoc in the countryside and which had always been an accomplice to a repressive Spanish state – particularly so under the autocratic Ferdinand VII. It was the sworn enemy of liberalism and hostile to the 1812 Constitution which directly challenged the Church's ideological and economic power.

Religious buildings were not the only targets for the fire-raisers. On subsequent days their attention turned to industry, and they set fire to La Bonaplata's El Vapor, the first large-scale industrial plant driven by steam, in the Raval. Since many of the rioters were workers, or at least would be seeking work in the new industries, their actions may seem contradictory. There is very little calculation involved in situations of violent confrontation. Many of these people were migrants from the countryside who had worked until recently in the small, artisan weaving shops outside the city. La Bonaplata symbolised, for them, both the possibility of a job and at the same time the collapse of their domestic weaving industry.

Like the Luddites in Britain, these were not enemies of modernity and industrialisation in a simple sense. In the specific conditions in which all this was occurring, they were also its victims.

Many of those involved in the fire-raising had emerged from the densely populated and insanitary streets on either side of the Ramblas, where the previous generation of textile workshops sat side by side with the living spaces of their workers.

The aftermath of the burning of churches was, perhaps surprisingly, the emergence from the rubble of new industries and factories – and the symbolic demolition of the city wall. A new Barcelona was emerging now: a city of expanding industries, in a Cataluña that was also undergoing change. A year after the church burnings, the new minister of finance, and later prime minister, Mendizábal, introduced a Law of Disentailment, ending the mortmain system that allowed religious institutions, among others, to own lands in perpetuity. The law suspended that right and decreed the expropriation of the 25 per cent of Cataluña's land owned by them. But if the intention was to sell off the land to a new class of small proprietors, it was not what happened. Instead the land in the Raval, for example, was divided into large plots which became the site of new industrial factories such as Guell's plant in Sants. A new social class, which had begun to emerge in the previous century, would now grow and stamp its mark on a much-changed city.

The Liceu theatre and the Boquería market arose on what had once been Church lands, as did the Plaza Reial in the Old Town. In the Raval the Boquería market, with its glorious cornucopia of fruit and vegetables, meats and cheeses, but most dramatically its central arc of stands where fish in their infinite variety lie on their ice beds until plucked from them by the elegant bejewelled women who sell them, is a magnet for Barcelonans as well as tourists today. It was previously an open market outside a Carmelite convent; once the convent was demolished, the current iron-framed building filled the space and only the smaller surrounding streets provide any hint of its past.

Barcelona is a city that has been asked – or told – to forget its past many times. It never has; instead it has reinvented itself over and over again. Each transformation, of course, has provoked controversy. The powerful trading city of medieval times lost its dominant position when the new Monarchs of Castile and Aragon decreed its exclusion from the profitable commerce with the Americas. In 1714, the city was almost destroyed and denied its language and its governing institutions. Yet a century later it was at the forefront of an industrial revolution. The victory of fascism in the Spanish Civil War once again denied Barcelona its language and its culture. Yet by the end of the twentieth century it was celebrating both in some spectacular ways.

The Ramblas played a part in each of these moments: as battlefield, promenade and theatre of the absurd.

As Giles Tremlett puts it in his *Ghosts of Spain* (2012), 'I know of no other city where a single street is so important [. . .] This is where Barcelona celebrates, protests and riots. Las Ramblas caters – in one way or another – for the most elemental desires of life.' Some years after his first stay in the city he returned at the beginning of the new century:

> Coming back I find the people have changed. There is more variety. I can hear Arabic and Urdu, most of the languages of Europe and others from Africa and Asia. Some of the castellano is spoken with Latin American accents. Barcelona, I realise, has become a city of immigrants. The Ramblas does not care. It is as noisy and busy as ever.

After all, it is that history and that diversity that have brought millions of visitors to Barcelona over the decades. In 2005, the second title on the list of the year's bestselling books was Carlos Ruiz Zafón's *The Shadow of the Wind* (2001), in which a young man uncovers the Cemetery of Forgotten Books, a discovery that launches him on a search through a Barcelona that is half-real and half-imaginary.

It would be nice to think that the present volume might set the traveller on his or her own search for a Barcelona of the imagination, a city that many writers have rediscovered over time. And that seems especially appropriate for a city where couples celebrate its patron saint, Sant Jordi or Saint George, every year on 23 April, by exchanging a book for a rose.

THE GOTHIC QUARTER: THE BARRI GÒTIC

The Secret Square

The Irish novelist Colm Tóibín spent a number of years living in Barcelona, a city he clearly loved and knew well. Katherine Proctor, the central character of his spare and sensitive novel *The South* (2015), abandons her home in Enniscorthy, in County Wexford, Ireland, to go south to Cataluña. Katherine leaves Ireland, its repressions and traumatic memories, to find a place where she can paint and find her own freedom. Her journey is as much an escape as it is a voyage of discovery and an exploration. Her search is for an artistic and personal space she has been unable to find amid the restrictions of her own life. Her family home was burned down by Republicans, and her relationships with her husband and son are suffocating and incommunicative. Her mother is an oppressive presence despite her abandonment of her own daughter. The restraints on Katherine are social, religious and historical. Her decision to move south is taken quietly but with resolution, whatever it is that awaits her there.

Much of the novel is set in a mountain village in the north of Cataluña, but she arrives first in Barcelona. She takes an evening walk through the Gothic Quarter, the Old Town.

> That night I found the real Barcelona for the first time. I had dinner in the Hotel Colón opposite the Cathedral and afterwards it was dark and I walked up by the church. I had not been this

way before. The streets were deserted and there were shadows everywhere cast by the lamps which shone from the walls. The stone of those buildings – the churches, the libraries and museums – was solid and thick. There was hardly anything modern; even the electric light from the walls resembled light from a torch. I found it overwhelming. Eventually I walked down a narrow passage I had thought was a cul-de-sac. The air was still warm and when I touched the stone I was shocked at how cold it was. I remember I stood there and I shivered. I was going to turn back but around the corner I could see an archway leading into the square so I kept on. There was a small fountain in the middle with two trees on either side. The trees had been pruned down to their essentials, gnarled branches which seemed deformed and grotesque like arms and legs with bits chopped off: it was impossible to imagine how they could grow again.

The curious thing about Barcelona, Tóibín writes in his *Homage to Barcelona* (2010), is that it has somehow been arrested in time. A trading centre as important as Genoa or Venice entered a sudden decline at the end of the fourteenth century, as power passed to Castile.

The medieval city was enclosed within a city wall, expanded twice by the late fourteenth century. Yet the wall remained in place until 1855. Thus, unlike other great cities of the era, it did not open out into wide avenues and grand squares, but remained a warren of dark, narrow streets. When the wall was finally demolished in the nineteenth century, new spaces opened – Carrer Ferran, a street of elegant shops, connected the Ramblas and Plaza Sant Jaume, while Plaza Reial, whose construction began in 1820 on the site of what had been a convent, was an elegant town square of cloisters and a fountain, whose street lamps would later be designed by a young architect called Antoni Gaudí, in 1870. The new spaces allowed some light to penetrate the inner city, but Sant Jaume was still the main square, where the Catalan government, the Generalitat, and the Barcelona City Council faced one another across the cobbles. The narrow streets into and out of the square led back into labyrinths of the Gothic Quarter. It was here that the population gathered to await the decision of the Consell de Cent, the Council of One Hundred, on whether to resist the siege of 1714; it was here that a packed crowd heard Francesc Macià announce the creation of a Catalan Republic in 1931. And in 2017 there was not a single space to be found when Carles Puigdemont again declared Catalan independence, before the government of Madrid imposed direct rule.

Katherine's walk had taken her into what had been the Jewish ghetto, the Call, and its atmospheric square of San Felipe Neri. Here the main synagogue had once stood; the body of the ghetto was demolished after the expulsion of the Jews in 1492 to give way to ecclesiastical buildings around the cathedral. San Felipe Neri retains an air of mystery; most visitors, like Katherine, probably

1 San Felipe Neri Square in the Gothic Quarter. It figures in Carlos Ruiz Zafón's novel The Shadow of the Wind *and Ildefonso Falcones'* Cathedral of the Sea

stumble on it, hidden in the maze of narrow streets. Carlos Ruiz Zafón described it too in his *The Shadow of the Wind*:

> Plaza San Felipe Neri is like a breathing space in the maze of streets that crisscross the Gothic Quarter, hidden behind the old Roman walls. The holes left by machine-gun fire during the war pockmark the church walls. That morning a group of children played soldiers, oblivious to the memory of the stones. A young woman, her hair streaked with silver, watched them from the bench where she sat with an open book on her lap and an absent smile. The address showed that Nuria Montfort lived in a building by the entrance to the square. The year of its construction was still visible on the blackened stone arch that crowned the front door. 1801.'

San Felipe Neri was bombed by Franco's planes in January 1938; 20 children died in the orphanage that occupied one side of the square.

The Gothic Quarter, the medieval city, has a double history – and its dividing point is the siege of Barcelona in 1714, although it would remain enclosed within its walls for a further 150 years.

The Cathedral of the Sea

Two recent highly successful historical novels have provided a sense of the medieval city – *Cathedral of the Sea* (2006) by Ildefonso Falcones and Albert Sánchez Piñol's *Victus* (2014). The Cathedral of Falcones' novel is Santa María del Mar, which sits in a small square not far from the Born market. It is an outstanding example of Catalan Gothic in its stark and austere interior; it is not to be confused with the Gothic façade of Barcelona's cathedral, which is in fact a kind of pastiche of a European Gothic style commissioned by a deeply religious, and very rich, businessman in the late nineteenth century.

2 Santa María del Mar, the Cathedral of the Sea

The area in which Santa María del Mar stands was incorporated into the city in the thirteenth century as the wall was extended, at the same time as the districts of Santa Catarina (where the old market was replaced by the modern structure designed by Enric Miralles) and Sant Pere, where the Palau de la Música was later built. The church, whose construction began in 1522 and took 50 years to complete, was dedicated to the Virgin of the Sea and built by the *bastaixos,* or longshoremen, using rocks carried bodily from the stone quarry on the hill of Montjuich. It was largely paid for by those who built it. A central theme of the novel is the process of its construction, to which the Falcones' main character, Arnau Estanyol, contributes directly.

The symbolic significance of the great church is 'its lasting reputation as a popular church, a building made for workers by workers' as Robert Hughes puts it in his book *Barcelona* (2001), though he adds with characteristic irony, 'that didn't prevent the anarchists from starting a fire in it during the Spanish civil war, destroying most of its accumulated ornaments and fittings'. But the stark grandeur of this iconic building seems all the more dramatic for its simplicity.

In his afterword to *Cathedral of the Sea*, Falcones tells us:

> Santa María del Mar is without doubt one of the most beautiful churches to be found anywhere. It may lack the monumentality of others built at the same time or later, but its interior is filled with the spirit with which Berenguer de Montagut [its architect, who figures in the novel] sought to infuse it: a people's church, built by the people of Barcelona for Barcelona, it is like an airy Catalan farmhouse. It is austere, protected and protecting, and the light of the Mediterranean sets it apart from any other church in the world.

The novel makes a character of the building, a focus and centre of the growing La Ribera district where it stands. It was certainly a busy and extremely prosperous city in the times Falcones describes, its activity and wealth drawing in immigrants from the countryside – though the city's administration was held firmly by the citizens represented by the Council of One Hundred. Citizenship was not open to just anyone; illegal immigrants had to escape the attention of the city's guards for a year and a day to win the right to remain. Arnau is brought to the city by his father after a confrontation with the local lord who had exercised his *droit de seigneur* with Arnau's mother. Father and son find unwilling refuge with the father's sister and brother-in-law, who exploit them mercilessly before eventually evicting them for fear that they will be caught and punished for harbouring an illegal immigrant. The father is crucified for a theft he did not commit and Arnau finds his way eventually to Santa María del Mar and the brotherhood of *bastaixos*, which he joins, having hauled his rock from Montjuich before his initiation. The girl he loves is denied to him in marriage because of his low status, though among workers the *bastaixos* were a strong and well-organised elite. The girl is married off to an elderly craftsman, but she and Arnau conduct a passionate secret love affair. Arnau in the meantime marries a beautiful and devoted young woman and joins the army of the Catalan King Pedro III in his war to recover the Catalan territories around the French border from his rival, the King of Mallorca. Arnau's decision is driven by his need to break the pattern of his love affair, because the strict rules of the *bastaixos'* guild will punish any of its members who commit adultery.

On his return, he finds a city riven by the plague, to which his wife eventually succumbs. The combination of an economic crisis brought on by the high cost of war and the plague drives frenzied crowds to attack the Call, the Jewish ghetto, blaming the Jews for the spread of the disease. The Jewish community of Barcelona was enclosed within the walls of the Call, but as the plagues devastated the population, it came under ferocious attack in 1348 and 1367, before the full-scale expulsion of the Jews from Spain in 1492. Some remains of the Call can still be found around Carrer Ferran or in the Gothic Quarter, while other parts lie beneath the Casa de la Ciutat and the Generalitat in the Plaza Sant Jaume. But it is probably the iconic little square of San Felipe Neri, and the narrow streets that lead there, that immediately evoke the sense of the ghetto. An attack there is described in *Cathedral of the Sea*:

> Arnau saw a mob of citizens blinded by hatred throw themselves wildly against the doors and walls of the Jewish quarter. There was no leader; the closest there came to an order were the screams of the flagellants who tortured themselves by the wall and incited the citizens to climb over and murder the heretics. Many fell to the swords of the king's soldiers when they reached the top, but the Jewish quarter was under attack from all four sides and others did manage to overwhelm the troops and make direct contact with the Jews.

A distracted Arnau simply walks on, absorbed in his own grief, until he sees the mob attacking three small children and their attendant, a North African slave:

> He had been taught to attack first and catch the opponent unawares. Arnau took out his knife and launched himself at the nearest attackers, to the shout of 'Sant Jordi'. He plunged the blade into the stomach of the first and then turned on the spot, forcing those behind him to back away. The knife scored the chest of several others, though one of those on the ground stuck his knife into Arnau's calf. Arnau looked at him, grabbed his hair, forced his head back and cut his throat.

He then takes the children and the servant to safety in the grounds of Santa María del Mar. The children prove to be the family of a wealthy Jewish moneylender, and the servant his highly knowledgeable collaborator. Arnau becomes his partner and grows rich very quickly. This allows him to buy up all the property of the members of his family who had humiliated and caused the death of his father, and to take his revenge, evicting them naked into the streets when their fortunes change.

The novel's cast of characters – tyrannical lords, honest workers, corrupt kings and merchants, the beautiful peasant girls, the camp followers and mercenary troops – are familiar elements of the historical novel. But for a contemporary reader the geography of the ancient city is still accessible, even if it has been transformed over time. For all the changes and alterations they have undergone, the Cathedral of the Sea itself, the Born market, the mansions still surviving in Carrer Montcada or Carrer Ample, and the institutions of the port built in the epoch the novel describes – the Llotja and the Consulat del Mar – still occupy important places in the contemporary city.

Arnau's closest friend, Joanet, whom he calls his brother, enters religious orders and becomes a fearsome prosecutor for the Inquisition, driven by a fundamentalist fervour as violent in its way as the actions of the *almogóvars*, the rural mercenaries famed for their wild courage and their merciless elimination of their enemies, which Falcones graphically describes.

The final part of Falcones' novel brings his hero Arnau face to face with the Inquisition. In the event, his charitable acts and contributions to the Church of Santa María make him a popular figure (despite his wealth) and he is rescued by the Barcelona mob to the cry of 'Visca fora', the traditional call to arms when the city is endangered. In the late 1300s, Barcelona's civil administration still controlled the life of the city and had sufficient authority to deny the Inquisition the exclusive power it would enjoy a century later. Even as late as 1483 the sinister Torquemada, head of the Inquisition, was refused entry to the city.

The period the novel describes marked the building of a new city wall and the enclosure of what had until then been an open stream flowing down to the sea along the outer perimeter. The new wall brought it within city limits and began its reconstruction as a walkway – the Ramblas now so central to the city's life. The city's expansion and importance were symbolised too in the building of the royal docks at Drassanes (now the Maritime Museum) at the port. By this time, the city's population had passed 40,000, and it was still expanding.

Just a few hundred yards from Santa María del Mar is the Born, a nineteenth-century iron structure that housed a major market and which today is a district of fashionable boutiques, bars and restaurants. The market itself, closed for a number of years, is now the elegant and informative Museum of the History of Barcelona. It makes an appearance in *Cathedral of the Sea* too:

> Early in the morning Arnau and Joan attended mass and joined the solemn processions that wound their way around the city accompanied by the sound of bells. Later, they followed the crowds wandering through the streets and enjoying the jousting and tournaments in the Born, where the nobility demonstrated their fighting skills, on foot and armed with great swords, or on horseback charging one another, their lances pointed directly at their opponents. The two boys were fascinated by the representations of naval battles. 'They look much bigger out of the water,' Arnau commented, pointing at the barges and galleons mounted on wheels that toured the city, while the sailors simulated boarding and attacks.

Nearly three centuries later, the Born area would be subject to a bombardment during the siege of 1714 – and then emerge like a phoenix from the ashes in the nineteenth-century rebuilding of the city.

In the sixteenth century Barcelona's days of prosperity were behind it. Yet when Miguel Cervantes had his eponymous hero Don Quixote and his squire Sancho Panza visit it in 1616, he described it as 'Barcelona, the treasure house of courtesy, haven of strangers, asylum of the poor, home of the valiant, champion of the wronged, pleasant exchange of firm friendships – a city unrivalled in location and beauty.' Given the living conditions in the crowded and insalubrious La Ribera district (where the Born stands), this seems a rather one-sided view, though it is confirmed in Enric Calpena's 2015 biography of the city, which he describes at the end of that century as 'a lively city, with a very rich social life, noisy and perfectly comparable to any of the principal European cities of the day', with its 40,000 free citizens and a significant population of servants and slaves.

In some real sense there were two Cataluñas at this time. There was Barcelona and its surrounding cities, governed from a Generalitat that claimed to represent all Catalans, although in fact it was controlled by the nobility and the merchant classes. In the inland areas of the country, however, the terrain was harsher and agriculture far more of a struggle. One writer described it as 'barbarous and primitive', and violence was endemic. A new aristocracy of big peasant farmers (*pageses grossos*) grew up alongside the smaller family farms run by the *masovers*. Beneath them, in this rigid hierarchy, were the landless poor peasantry who worked for both.

In the Pyrenees the fiefdoms of local aristocrats persisted outside the control of the viceregency or the Corts. Their conflicts and rivalries produced a Cataluña divided between *nyerros* and *cadells*, defined by their allegiance to one section of the nobility over another, and their perpetual war shaped the region for two centuries. There was little difference between them; they were simply supporters of opposing factions. Their conflict sustained the atmosphere of violence and fear in the countryside and certainly fuelled the emergence of banditry as a major problem throughout the region as the seventeenth century began. In fact, after praising Barcelona, Sancho Panza expresses some trepidation about a local bandit called Roca Guinarda, a Robin Hood figure who robbed the wealthy to help the poor – a rare attitude among rural bandits at the time.

Madrid had its own representative in Barcelona, the viceroy, just as it did in all of its external colonies; he was not a popular figure.

Few Catalans spoke Castilian Spanish, Cataluña had been excluded from the benefits of empire, and Madrid was constantly looking for finance from the Catalan banking sector. The unwilling always paid late and as little as they could. The relationship between Madrid and Barcelona was always conflictive, and the successive crises and conflicts of the first half of the seventeenth century simply deepened the rift. What is called the Thirty Years War in Europe, which followed the disintegration of the Holy Roman Empire, was in many ways the beginning of a century of almost continuous conflict which culminated, for Barcelona, in the devastating siege of the city in 1714 so powerfully represented in Albert Sánchez Piñol's novel *Victus*.

Wars are an expensive business, especially if they drag on for 30 years. The response of Spain's regent, the Count Duke of Olivares, was to demand contributions from every region of Spain, including Cataluña. When the Catalans baulked at the demand, Olivares sent 26,000 troops through the principality to fight the French at the northern frontier. What they encountered en route was a deep and bitter hostility, and what was effectively a guerrilla war as the Castilian troops wreaked havoc on their way. There was little love lost between them, in any event. The poet and satirist Francisco de Quevedo, who was prone to leaving vicious satirical sonnets under the plates of his dinner guests, gave no quarter to the Catalans. Just before his death, in 1645, he published his vituperative pamphlet 'The Rebellion of Barcelona':

> The Catalans kneel down and raise the left hand and put it together with a wooden one so that, while looking pious, they can steal with the right [. . .] They're like a pox on their rulers; they all suffer them, and those that escape infection are still left with their mark [. . .] and these pestilent people have the temerity to suggest to his majesty that he should change his ministers!

Plague had again ravaged the rural and urban population from 1629 to 1631. And in 1640, a confrontation in Carrer Ample in Barcelona between the reapers, or *segadors,* who were in the city waiting to be contracted, and the representatives of the Count Duke of Olivares, erupted into a full-scale revolt in which neither side gave any quarter. The rural guerrillas, or *miquelets,* exacted a merciless revenge from the Spanish armies. The Catalan revolt is commemorated every time the Catalans sing their national anthem, 'Els Segadors'.

Catalunya triomfant
tornarà a ser rica i plena.
Endarrera aquesta gent
tan ufana i tan superba.

Tornada:
Bon cop de falç!
Bon cop de falç,
defensors de la terra!
Bon cop de falç!

Ara és hora, segadors.
Ara és hora d'estar alerta.
Per quan vingui un altre juny,
esmolem ben bé les eines.
Tornada

Que tremoli l'enemic,
en veient la nostra ensenya.
Com fem caure espigues d'or,
quan convé seguem cadenes.
Tornada

Cataluña will be victorious
Be rich and bountiful once more
Let us drive out the
Arrogant and the self-important

Chorus:
Strike with your sickle
Strike with your sickle
Defend your land
And strike with your sickle.

Now is the time, reapers,
Time to be ready and alert
If another June should come
Let our tools be sharp.
Chorus

Let the enemy tremble
At the sight of our banner
Just as we cut the ears of golden wheat
When the times demand it, we cut through chains
Chorus

Barcelona Besieged

The rivalries of the previous century exploded again in 1701, when the War of Spanish Succession began. Once again it placed Cataluña in a kind of no man's land between rival monarchs. The specific spark was the death of the last Habsburg king of Spain, a very grand title for the poor disabled boy who was Charles II, heir to Philip IV. Charles was incapable of rule, and his vast empire was administered by his mother and a series of favourites. But even she was unable to force him to produce an heir to the throne, and in 1700, on his deathbed, Charles nominated the Bourbon candidate, Philip of Anjou, a grandson of Louis XIV of France, as his successor. For the rest of Europe's crowned heads, the chilling prospect was an alliance between France and Spain that would dominate the whole continent. So they (Austria, England, the Netherlands,

Sweden and others) found an alternative candidate for the Spanish Crown, the Austrian Prince Charles, heir to the Habsburgs. Having suffered Madrid's oppressive rule, the Catalans elected to throw in their lot with the anti-Bourbon alliance. Once again the cities and countryside of Cataluña would be trampled underfoot by foreign troops fighting a proxy war.

Alberto Sánchez Piñol's novel *Victus* provides an often heart-stopping narrative of these events, through the adventures and misadventures of a historical character Martí Zuviría, reimagined by the author and given a voice that is at once enraged, witty, insightful and historically sensitive. The narrative is his account of the events leading to the siege of Barcelona in 1714, as told to a curmudgeonly Austrian scribe when Martí is in his final years.

A Catalan, Martí gives a lacerating portrait of the relationship between Cataluña and Castile:

Castile's high point came with the conquest of the Americas. Thereafter it fell into a dull and lethargic stupor. An outcome written in its roots. The Castilian character par excellence is the *hidalgo*, that is, the nobleman, a medieval creation who still lives on. Proud to the point of madness, going out of his way for the sake of honour, capable of fighting to the death over a slight, but incapable of any constructive initiative. That which for him is a heroic gesture, in the eyes of a Catalan is nothing but the most laughably pig-headed error. He can't see beyond the present moment; like dragonflies, he aspires to brilliance but his wings flutter erratically, carrying him low and to no place in particular. He does not understand, much less tolerate, other ways of life. Industriousness is repellent to him.

Interestingly, Martí is a young man trained to become a military engineer by one of the great figures in the field, the French Royal Engineer Sebastian le Prêtre Marquis de Vauban. By accident and good fortune, and a heavy dose of sheer pragmatism, Martí learns his trade at the feet of the master and his wonderful twin assistants, the brothers Ducroix, and discovers his sexuality in the bed (well actually in the hayloft) of Vauban's beautiful and wise daughter Jeanne. His position as an engineer would later enable Martí to move between armies and allegiances, since he is employed as a technician and approaches the business of attack and defence with equal passion and skill, as his master had taught him, as well as having a professional pride, irrespective of who his employers are.

There is a familiar character in Spanish literature – the *pícaro* – that Martí represents. He is a survivor, amoral and pragmatic, who will change sides and allegiances at the drop of a hat. All he has is his wit and ingenuity, and an extraordinary instinct for survival. In Martí's case he is also an engineer, whose considerable skills can be put at the service of any master. Yet beneath the hard surface Martí has an ethical position – loyalty to his brotherhood and to his profession and, buried deep, a sense of his Catalan identity. When his complicated and risk-filled life brings him back to the Barcelona he left as a child, that identity is reawoken:

> I had left Barcelona as a boy and I was returning a man. A failure, but a man. I can assure you, this voice speaking to you now has never known a more frivolous port or a city, nor one that was home to more foreigners. Not even in America! They came, they settled, and their origins melted into the crowd. The day they decided to stay, they'd Catalanize their family names as a disguise, so nobody might know whether their birthplace had been in Italy, France, Castile or somewhere more exotic still. As for the rest, and in contrast to the Castilian obsession with keeping the blood pure of Moors or Jews, the Catalans didn't care a fig for their neighbour's origins. If they had money to spend, if they were pleasant enough, and if they didn't try and impose religious ideas, new arrivals were left to get on with it. This atmosphere, so passive and receptive, meant that the people would be transformed in less than a generation. So it was with my father.

Martí finds himself in Barcelona in 1713, just as the balance of forces in the war has changed. The death of the English Queen Anne and of Charles's older brother Joseph, Emperor of Austria, persuades Charles to assume the imperial role of the Habsburgs, while France and Spain, growing weary of the war, agree that Philip should retain the Spanish crown. Cataluña, abandoned now by its allies, is left alone to face the joint Spanish and French bombardment from the sea. The rulers of the city, the wealthy nobility, the 'red pelts' or the 'lickspittles in astrakhan' are happy to give in and escape. As the three branches of the Generalitat meet in Plaza Sant Jaume, their carriages await to take them to safety. The Church too favours surrender.

That was our worst defect, not knowing what we wanted beyond staying in our small stockade. Not this, but not that either. Neither France nor Spain, yet unable to build our own political edifice. Neither resigned to our fate nor willing to change it. Trapped between the jaws of France and Spain, we were content to ride the storm, and float like driftwood. Our ruling classes, particularly, were the height of chronic indecision, always somewhere between servility and resistance.

But the third branch of Catalan society, the people, stand in the square awaiting the decision – silent, determined – for two days and three nights.

In my opinion that was the real turning point. Not an act of rebellion but a deaf noncompliance. The people down there were so disconcerted by what they had heard, just as the nobles up on the balcony were disconcerted by the mass stillness and silence. What could they do? They couldn't expel all these people. Nobody would dare, nor did they have enough troops to try. Besides, an act of violence like that could lead to just the kinds of disturbance that the Red Pelts were trying so hard to avoid.

That whole night nobody moved from the packed square. The following day the people's branch of the parliament assembled. The atmosphere out on the street, and Ferrer's speech, had so fired them up that their vote went in favour of resistance, and by an overwhelming majority. This time the Plaza Sant Jaume did react, with an explosion of joy. 'Publish the Crida! Publish it!'

Martí, meanwhile, waits in his room in the La Ribera district in the company of his lover Amelis, and the three constant companions he has gathered around him on his journey:

Amelis took me to La Ribera, one of the most insalubrious and overpopulated neighbourhoods in all Barcelona, which is saying something. Solid grey buildings, three, four even five storeys high, and narrow little alleys that stopped the sunlight reaching ground level. It was unbelievably full of people and animals. Stray dogs, chickens living on balconies, milking goats tied to rings in the wall [. . .] Some of the people living there seemed quite content; they smoked and played dice in the doorways, using a barrel as a table. Others were like the living dead. I watched one man who looked like Saint Simeon the Stylite, the difference being that Simeon spent thirty years on top of a pillar and this man seemed to have been through at least double that, and living on a diet of sparrow shit.

The bombardment of the city – 27,275 bombs fell on the city in July and August 1713 – served only to strengthen the resolve of those resisting the siege, and to reinforce the determination of the commander of the besieging forces, James Fitzherbert, Duke of Berwick, with whom Martí – in a series of complex turns of fate – has had a relationship (they have briefly been lovers).

While the 'red pelts' have taken refuge on Montjuich, the population of La Ribera has little option other than resistance. And they resist heroically as the district is gradually reduced to rubble and its population live through increasing privations.

The novel ends with a moving description of the city's final days, before it falls on 11 September 1714. The heroes of the final battle are undoubtedly the ordinary people, the poor, the citizens. Their rulers have, with honourable exceptions, proved to be concerned only with their own survival; their priests could produce merely a set of last-minute rules 'to allay the Divine Fury', which seemed to consist largely of multiple passes of the rosary and a moral campaign against prostitution. But in the end, as Martí and his historical contemporaries well knew, it was not divine fury but the merciless revenge of Philip V of Spain from which they had most to fear. The Spanish King's letter to Berwick makes clear what he expects of his victorious commander:

> Any grace you may offer shall be no more than an act of pity. To those who, repenting of their error, ask for mercy before the walls are breached, you shall not offer it (but consider it only), reminding them of their rebellion and how unworthy they are of mercy, you may leave them in hope of it, offering to intercede with me so that their lives at least may be saved, the exception from this grace (which you shall only offer, no more) are the principal leaders.

Philip immediately imposed a punitive tax (the *cadastro*) on the city and banned the Catalan language. The university was closed and moved to a different location, at a distance from Barcelona. Thousands of refugees left the city for the north. (All of this would be repeated with Franco's occupation of the city in 1939.) The city was also placed under Castilian military occupation, and its physical organisation transformed to facilitate their domination. Among the many petty humiliations Catalans were subject to, no household was permitted to possess more than one knife, and that must be chained to the hearth.

The immediate cost of the siege was 7,000 Catalan lives, and more than double that number of Bourbon troops. The Catalans were buried in El Fossar de les Moreres, a mass grave which lies

3 *The monument that commemorates La Diada, 11 September 1714, when Barcelona was occupied. Crowds gather here every year on that day in the square in front of Santa María del Mar*

underneath the square beside the Church of Santa María del Mar. An eternal flame now burns there on a monument that bears a poem by Frederic Soler, declaring, 'No traitors are buried here, in the Fossar de les Moreres.' Each year on La Diada, Cataluña's National Day, 11 September, crowds gather there to commemorate the events of 1714.

The most brutal and hated symbol of Barcelona's defeat was the Ciutadella fortress, where the Parc de la Ciutadella and the Barcelona Zoo now stand. It was built to the Marquis of Verboom's design – the engineer whom Martí claimed to have murdered in *Victus* – though his original plan was even more extensive than the eventual building and was amended. Even so, it occupied one-fifth of the city, covering the area of the district of La Ribera, where Barcelona's poor had lived their crowded lives, which was demolished to accommodate the fortress. It had borne the brunt of the 1714 assault. The Ciutadella oversaw the city, and the razing of La Ribera left a free flight path for the missiles launched from its cannons. From the other side, Montjuich's artillery could fulfil the same function.

For a contemporary visitor it is difficult to imagine the city before the ugly fort dominated its coastal horizon. In the pavement on the avenue leading from the Arc de Trionf to the gates of the Ciutadella Park, there is a plan of the city as it was before the siege. By a fortunate accident it has become possible to walk the demolished streets once again and gather a sense of that city that Piñol describes.

The Born

The original square where the Born now stands was, as we have seen, the location of celebrations and rituals from medieval times. It was destroyed to make way for the Ciutadella. The present Born market was built between 1884 and 1886, its iron structure – among the first to be built wholly of that metal in the city – was forged at the La Maquinista and the Vulcan plants in Poble Nou, north of the Ciutadella. It was an imposing structure, the material expression of a confident merchant class whose wealthier members could satisfy their search there for the widest variety of fruit, vegetables, fish and meat at its 726 stalls. It certainly resembled its Parisian equivalents, the arcades (and their phantasmagoria) so vividly and precisely described by Walter Benjamin. The nearby Santa Catalina market served a different clientele but was its contemporary.

In *Victus* Martí's companion Nan performs in the Born square for the public in the midst of the siege. In those times it was known as the Plaza Mayor and was entirely surrounded by buildings. The bombardment after 1714 destroyed many of the streets and buildings around it, or so it was assumed. Abandoned in the 1960s, the Born was closed and stood empty for some years, until it was taken over by Barcelona's newest university, Pompeu Fabra. The building of an underground car park (which is still there) exposed architectural remains beneath the square, and the excavation revealed the remnants of some of the streets and houses of the La Ribera district. These have been fully exposed and there are guided tours around the streets and houses which are now part of a remarkable and very beautiful Cultural Centre, opened in 2013, which offers a regular programme of events and exhibitions – not to mention an excellent restaurant specialising in Catalan cuisine (each dish refers to some element of the siege). While the rest of the area was levelled in the building of the Ciutadella, and its population removed to the beach area which became the Barceloneta, the streets and dwellings in this part remained beneath the market building. Their survival may be due to the fact that they lie in a depression below the level of the surrounding streets. What we know is that the demolition ended here. The house at number 16, Paseo de Born, opposite the museum entrance, has curious half-windows that suggest that the demolition ended with its neighbours.

The Born district has been transformed by the modernisation of Barcelona. The museum itself is an imposing and fascinating historical space. But what was once an area of mixed housing, with grand mansions coexisting with crowded tenements, has undergone a slow metamorphosis. It is now a highly fashionable place to see and be seen. The cobbled square is surrounded by restaurants, trendy cafés and boutiques. Santa María del Mar is a stone's throw away, as is the Picasso Museum at Carrer Montcada. The Ciutadella, or what exists of it after its nineteenth-century transformation, remains close by with its park and zoo. Its cannons, however, have been definitively silenced.

3

THE CITY OF MARVELS

Before the Fires

The Ciutadella as it is today represents only a small part of the fortress whose construction began just two years after the siege of Barcelona, to house 5,000 soldiers. Its purpose was not the defence of the city itself, but the intimidation of the civilian population – such of it that remained there, since thousands had already fled. Its completion had cost the demolition of the La Ribera district, the centre of popular resistance in 1713–14, and of its 1,144 houses and its 38 streets.

Jacint Verdaguer, Catalunya's most important Romantic poet, recalled the humiliation of his city in his poem 'To Barcelona':

> Still stained with blood, and roaring like a beast
> The king went down into La Ribera
> Leading his grenadiers.
> 'Put down your swords,' he said, 'take rakes and hoes,
> Tear down these ancient houses
> Where bandits find their refuge.'
>
> And all around lie the grand houses
> Monasteries, schools and hospices,
> The churches and the hospital,
> Rows of slums lie scattered on the beach
> And the happiest of Barcelona's places
> Is now erased and buried in the sand.

That 'happy place' was the beach area, the Barceloneta, that Falcones described in *Cathedral of the Sea*. Some of the inhabitants of the La Ribera district were eventually moved to a rebuilt Barceloneta, originally designed by Verboom, the engineer responsible for the Ciutadella, though construction only began in 1753. The houses were in low two-storey blocks, with entry from both sides to allow ventilation, and ranged along straight streets built at right angles to one another. The area was also designed with social control in mind, immediately visible as it was from the castle walls, but also low enough not to be endangered by missiles fired from above.

The triangular spit of land, some of it reclaimed from the sea, was largely occupied until the eighteenth century by lean-tos and shanties where the fisher population lived. The sea was dangerous and the pollution of the beaches notorious. The residents of La Ribera who moved there lived largely from the sea at first, but by the mid-eighteenth century, and despite the continuing repression, the city's economic recovery was beginning. The emerging cotton industry contributed to Barcelona's renewed foreign trade; by the time Barceloneta was rebuilt, 10,000 people were employed in the industry. Barceloneta grew with it, as workers gravitated towards the area. The original design of the area, with only one in ten houses above two storeys, was quickly left behind. By the end of the century, according to Calpena, nine out of ten buildings were four storeys high, and many of the original dwellings were now subdivided to accommodate the labourers arriving from the provinces and the south.

In 1776, Henry Swinburne described a visit to the city in his *Travels Through Spain in 1775 and 1776*:

In Barcelona, no-one is allowed to carry arms in the street and discipline is strict. Among other restrictions, the wearing of wide-brimmed hats and long dark capes is forbidden. Until recently no-one dared to carry a knife and in the restaurants there was one chained to the table for the use of customers. You can walk the

streets at any hour unarmed and without fear, as long as you carry
a lantern, because without one you may be stopped by a patrol.
One end of the wall connects to the Ramblas, a long irregular
avenue that is beginning to be straightened and widened. There
ladies parade in their carriages or sometimes tour the city along
the walls, that are brick and were recently repaired and improved.

The city was rebuilt at first to eliminate the iconic pre-siege
buildings, in particular churches and monasteries associated
with the rebellion. The Llotja, the commercial exchange, began
its metamorphosis in 1764, the customs building in 1790. The
renewed façades, Neoclassical in style, symbolised the new phase in
the city's growth. The Conde de Asalto was responsible for one of
the more far-sighted projects of urban renewal, the building of the
Ramblas and the extension of the Raval, one of whose main streets
was named after him. The Ramblas at that stage principally served
to give access to the religious houses that had arisen on the other
side of the stream, in the area later called the Raval. The rebuilding
of the Ramblas, and of the Raval district, began in 1776, gradually
transforming the serpentine and uneven paths beside the polluted
Cagallel into the wide, straight boulevard which by the following
century, and until the present, became the main avenue through
old Barcelona, its wide central pavement providing a stage for all
the city's inhabitants, rich and poor, permanent and transient, to
see and be seen.

Like Baron Haussmann's reconstruction of Paris in the wake of
the Paris Commune of 1871, as Walter Benjamin's wonderful *Paris,
Capital of the Nineteenth Century* (1933) describes, the wide avenue
had a dual purpose – not simply to modernise but also to replace
some of the all too easily barricaded narrow streets of the old city and
to provide immediate access for military incursions when necessary.
As Robert Hughes puts it in *Barcelona*, 'the Gothic Quarter was the
natural terrain for urban guerrillas, while the Ramblas, implicitly,
represented the supremacy of the army.'

Barcelona's new prosperity and its economic growth had produced an expanded class of wealthy merchants, the first generation of whom were the beneficiaries of the Atlantic trade. These were the *indianos*, those who had grown wealthy on Atlantic commerce and the slave trade of the Indies. It was a name already given, with very little complimentary intent, to those who returned rich from the colonies. It could equally have been applied to Daniel Defoe's Moll Flanders, who grew rich in the colonies, had she relocated to Spain! In Barcelona and its surrounding countryside there are tell-tale signs of the presence of *indianos*. Look for a tall palm tree or two at the threshold of one of the grand country houses (the *masías*) that pepper the rural space. These trees are not native to Cataluña but were brought back on the trading ships from the Caribbean. As the city expanded, these newly (and enormously) wealthy returnees built their palaces on the Ramblas, each bearing the name of the family who occupied it. The Casa March de Reus and the Palau Mojá look directly on to the Ramblas; the Palau Serra is on Carrer Ample, off the Ramblas at the harbour end. We have already heard the story of notorious Viceroy Amat's Palacio de la Virreina and of the Palacio Guell, built by Gaudí.

Their wealth was invested in Cataluña itself, in the textile 'factories' in the La Ribera district and towards the end of the century in the Raval. Antonio de Capmany's monumental five-volume *Memorias históricas sobre la marina, comercio y artes de la antigua ciudad de Barcelona* (*Historical Memoir of the Navy, Commerce and Arts of the Ancient City of Barcelona*), published in 1779 (but not available in English), makes an impassioned claim for Barcelona's leading place in the history of seaborne commerce and in the growth of industry in the peninsula. He notes, for instance, with a nice sense of irony, that just 15 years after the siege of 1714, the occupying troops were dressed in locally made fabrics, which in earlier times would have been imported from Italy or Holland. The first factory of printed fabrics opened in 1737; within 30 years the number of plants had jumped to 20. And by the century's end some

18,000 people were employed in the manufacture of cotton cloth, and 12,000 in the production of silk. The port of Barcelona was receiving on average 1,100 vessels per year. Its population, reduced to 37,000 in 1717, reached 134,000 by 1798.

By any standards it was a city reborn from its own ashes. Yet, as the century ended, Cataluña once again became a field of battle for wider forces. In 1793, France declared war on Spain in La Guerra Gran (The Major War). Driven back at the battle of Peristortes, the French army crossed the Pyrenees again and took the coastal town of Figueres (home now to the Dalí Museum). But the French did not push on to Barcelona; they were driven back by the guerrilla forces and, amid general disgust, Spain signed a treaty of alliance with France in 1795. This provoked an English naval blockade, whose effect was to paralyse the American trade and cause an economic crisis in the city which would drag on for 30 years before Barcelona embarked on yet another process of recovery.

The French returned in 1807; the Peninsular Wars and their characteristic cruelty were dramatically illustrated in Goya's *Dos de Mayo* series of engravings. Napoleon's invasion of Spain was resisted by an alliance of England, Portugal and a Spain now ruled by the absolutist Ferdinand VII. He abdicated and in 1812 the Cortes (the Spanish parliament) passed a liberal constitution. Ferdinand returned in 1813 to a Spain whose imperial rule in the Americas was coming to an end as Latin American independence movements spread, ending three centuries of Spanish imperial domination. His first act was to declare the constitution null and void and to restore the Inquisition. To describe a complex situation in simple terms, Spain (and Cataluña) were now divided between liberals, mainly confined to the cities, and conservative forces supporting Ferdinand but largely led by the most conservative elements of the Catholic Church. After Ferdinand's death, the reactionaries shifted their support to the discarded pretender to the throne, Don Carlos. These were the Carlists, who waged war in the Catalan countryside for the next 20 years.

Revenge by Fire

The fire-raising of 1835, to which we have already made reference, was in a sense a crossroads in the city's history. The summer that July was especially hot, and the resentments built up during the various occupations of the city by foreign troops – especially during the years when the Comte d'Espagne, renowned for his cruelty and violent repression, was there as the representative of the Spanish Crown – were at bursting point. Barcelona was crowded with refugees from the rural violence, and with workers who had abandoned small-scale domestic production in the interior to seek work in the city's factories. Many of them had firsthand experience of the Carlist violence still causing ravages in the interior. Whatever the case, the Church and its advocates were the enemy of liberal Barcelona, and the crowds went on a rampage through the city.

On 27 July, the day after the violence at the bullring, General Llauder arrived in the city to put down the riot, but when a large crowd gathered menacingly outside his headquarters, he elected to take refuge in the Ciutadella. In subsequent days, the burnings spread across Cataluña. On 5 August General Bassa was dispatched from Madrid at the head of a detachment of Spanish troops, but he was caught and killed and his body, like the unfortunate bull before him, dragged through the streets. It was on the same day that crowds surrounded and set fire to the La Bonaplata. Bonaplata himself tried to defend the factory, but failed; he fell into a deep depression and died soon afterwards.

On 7 August General Pastor launched a fierce campaign of repression; seven workers were shot and killed and hundreds more injured and arrested. The rebellion had been crushed for the moment, but the seething discontent among the poor and underpaid in the disease-ridden slums of the old city continued to boil, and the additional burden of the *burots*, taxes on all products entering the walled city, was the final straw. New protests erupted in November 1842. General Espartero, who had taken over the regency from the queen two years earlier, had a ruthless reputation. He demanded that all participants in the rebellion lay down their arms, and when they refused, he surrounded the Gothic Quarter and bombarded it from Montjuich and the Ciutadella. Over 400 houses were destroyed. Etienne Cabet, the author of *Travels in Icaria,* witnessed the bombing and described it in his *Bombardment of Barcelona* (1843):

> The two hospitals have been destroyed; twelve bombs fell on one of them. The residence of the French Consul was attacked by bombs and bullets, despite the fact that he had raised the flag and it could be seen clearly from the fortress. The main streets are impassable because of the accumulation of debris. Many houses have been burned down.

In 1843 a new rebellion, La Jamancia, held the city for several months under the control of the local volunteer militia, until it too was bombed into submission, this time at the hands of General Prim (whose statue, ironically, still stands within the Ciutadella Park). At the same time, the city's expansion and transformation were progressing. The construction of the Ramblas and the first streets of the Raval incorporated the excluded and marginal areas into the city proper. The burned-out convents and churches and the expropriated Church lands provided virgin plots for the new building. The Plaza Reial had been a Capuchin convent; the Boquería market, now so emblematic of Barcelona, was built as a permanent structure where a Carmelite convent had once been. The theory had been that the release of the lands would bring in small-scale individual proprietors, but, as already mentioned, in fact it was the city's wealthy families who bought them.

The *indianos* were moving actively into a modern, capitalist economy. The father of Eusebi Guell, Juan, set up an industrial plant building textile machinery at La Máquina Terrestre y Marítima (Machinery of Land and Sea) in 1855. Joan Xifré, who had made his fortune in tanning, built his residential block, Parxos d'en Xifré, overlooking the harbour on the Paseo Colón. Many of the people had emigrated to the Raval or La Ribera to work in the factories – but their resentment obviously continued to bubble beneath the surface.The industrial landscape was changing rapidly, and in the Raval, Barceloneta, Poble Nou and in Sants, the working-class inner suburbs of Barcelona, new factories were following the lead of Bonaplata's El Vapor. This was now a mechanised industry, using the spinning jennies and the flying shuttles to transform what had been a home-based trade into a fully fledged modern industry whose machinery was also manufactured within the city, at the Nuevo Volcan foundry in the Barceloneta, La España Industrial in Sants (founded in 1849, now a park), and the most important, Guell's La Maquinista Terrestre y Marítima. Barcelona's first railway, the line to Mataró, was inaugurated in 1848 with four locomotives brought from Britain, while the burgeoning overseas trade stimulated the port. By the mid-nineteenth century it was estimated that the annual traffic there amounted to over 7,700 ships and over 400,000 tons of merchandise – raw cotton and coal brought in, textiles, aguardiente (sometimes more elegantly described as cognac, a very popular import to the Americas) sent abroad. The city's population had reached 180,000 by then; and 33 per cent of them worked in the cotton industry's 60 factories and 800 small workshops. And yet, for all the modernisation of the industry, disease swept through the poor districts again and again during those years.

The city walls were an obvious anachronism in the new Barcelona. The issues that prevailed in its social and political life were increasingly concerned with the conflicting interests of merchants and workers, as the former pursued profits and returns on investment and the latter began to organise collectively to defend their common interests. The renewed struggles over mechanisation led to the creation of an effective trade union in 1854, and in 1855 its leader, Josep Barceló, was executed on a trumped-up charge. The result was the city's first general strike, which was put down by the captain general – still the ultimate military authority in the city – and trade unions were made illegal.

Popular demonstrations were often led by the slogan 'A terra les muralles' ('Down with the walls'), a suffocating imprisoning barrier both symbolically and materially. The riots of 1842 – known as the *bullangas* – were essentially risings of the urban poor, but they were also the first, if disordered, expression of a nascent trade unionism.

The Eixample

In 1855, it was finally agreed by Madrid that the old city walls should come down, and demolition began two years later. The city authorities launched a competition for the design of a new town, or an expansion plan – the Eixample. There were two entries, one presented by Rivera i Trias and the second by Ildefons Cerdà, a highway engineer. The Barcelona authorities chose Rivera i Trias's project, which envisaged a Barcelona that looked very like Vienna. To their astonishment, they were overruled by the Madrid government, who imposed Cerdà's plan instead. It was a curious decision and the most convincing explanation for it – other than the sheer pleasure of contradicting Barcelona – was that the government at the time contained an unusually large number of engineers. The decision is all the more surprising because Cerdà's urban plan was radical and progressive for its time, and clearly influenced by Etienne Cabet's notions of an organised and egalitarian community placed in a humane and healthy environment.

Etienne Cabet's *Travels in Icaria: A Journey to Utopia*, first published in 1840, was widely read among Barcelona's radicals of the time. A Utopian socialist narrative, it described a cooperative community of equals, though to a modern reader its rules and structures seem rigid and hierarchical. But for people such as Narcís Monturiol, Cabet was a visionary of a future society. Monturiol's newspaper, *La Fraternidad*, disseminated his ideas, although their subversive content led to his expulsion from the city. He went into hiding in Figueres, where he conceived the idea for which he is remembered today – the submersible or submarine he called *Ictíneo,* commemorated now in the park opposite the Aquarium. He did eventually build and test his craft in 1859 in the waters of Barcelona's port. His achievement, while not widely recognised beyond Cataluña, is commemorated in the Maritime Museum in the Atarazanas, once the royal dockyards, that overlook the port. It has been suggested that Jules Verne, an enthusiastic follower of technical and scientific innovations everywhere, may well have taken Monturiol as the model for the Captain Nemo of *20,000 Leagues Under the Sea*, especially as Nemo is much given to speeches reminiscent of the Utopian socialism of Cabet.

As Nemo explains in Verne's novel:

The sea is the vast reservoir of Nature. The globe began with sea, so to speak; and who knows if it will not end with it? In it is supreme tranquillity. The sea does not belong to despots. Upon its surface men can still exercise unjust laws, fight, tear one another to pieces, and be carried away with terrestrial horrors. But at thirty feet below its level, their reign ceases, their influence is quenched, and their power disappears. Ah! Sir, live – live in the bosom of the waters! There only is independence! There I recognise no masters! There I am free!

Cerdà, a close friend of Monturiol's, was a fellow enthusiast for Cabet's ideas. Born in a country house in the heart of Cataluña, Cerdà and his family moved to Vic in flight from the Carlist wars. He went on to study in Madrid, moving to Barcelona in 1849, where he was politically active, and a vigorous advocate of the demolition of the city walls.

Cerdà's plan proposed an open-ended expansion divided north-west to south-east, and south-west to north-east by long straight avenues 20 metres wide; each city block (or *manzana*) would be a

4 Ramon Martí's portrait of Ildefons Cerdà, architect of the Eixample

square 113.3 metres long on each side. The district would be crossed in turn by five much wider avenues, two perpendicular (Paseo de Gracia and Avinguda de las Corts Catalans) and three diagonal (Diagonal, Paralelo and La Meridiana). His original idea was that there would be buildings only on two sides of each block, leaving the rest for gardens and open spaces. The blocks would be organised in groups, each containing schools, churches, social centres and nurseries. Tree-lined avenues and regular parks reinforced this concept of a garden city, regimented perhaps, but guaranteeing light, air and a healthy environment. It was without question a utopian project and a visionary one. Sadly, Cerdà's plan was realised in a very different spirit, dominated by speculators who shared none of his ideas. It is especially ironic that a colleague of Cerdà's, Pere García Faria, a public health specialist, added an equally visionary plan for public health, water provision and waste disposal based on a survey of living conditions in the city. That too was ignored. In the end, the blocks were built on all four sides and in many cases

without the minimum sewage facilities inherent to the plan. The four-storey limit to the height of buildings was also ignored.

The task of naming the streets was given to Victor Balaguer, a writer and nationalist. His Catalanism is evident in the names he chose, all of which refer to aspects of Cataluña's traditions and history, like the Corts Catalans, la Diputació or its past heroes such as Roger de Flor. For Cerdà, the fate of his plan at the hands of the surging capitalist class of builders and proprietors was a bitter disappointment and he died poor and disillusioned.

At the end of 1869, the Ciutadella finally came down too, and was transformed into a public park. Three years later, the first trams began to run along the Paseo de Gracia, the grand central avenue of the Eixample. Yet the reality was that the Eixample developed slowly; major building work began only in the 1880s, financed by the 'gold fever' of the previous decade. A glance along the Paseo de Gracia shows buildings of varying heights; the taller they are, the later they were built, as Cerdà's original plan had imposed a maximum height of four storeys.

The Eixample today is much admired on the tourist route. The main crowds are on the Paseo de Gracia, where the key buildings of the Modernisme movement are to be found – and today the majority of high-end luxury clothes and jewellery stores as well. A walk down any of the lateral streets will take the visitor past striking carved doorways through whose elaborate glass panels can be seen marble hallways and curved stairs snaking around wood-panelled elevators. The area was certainly a byword for elegance and luxury. But the speculators had not only ignored Cerdà's plan, they also set aside Pere García Faria's public health project. Cerdà's utopian vision of a safe, planned city had been driven aside by the speculators in the frenzy of the gold fever. The 1,000 families who occupied the area by the end of the 1870s would have been less than comfortable. The lack of proper sewers was an assault on public health and in the summer the area was rife with malaria. In fact, disease may have been the only thing that every social class had in common.

Gold Fever

The Republic fell in 1875 and the monarchy returned under Isabel's son Alfonso XII. It would initiate the period known as the 'febre d'or' (gold fever), when the repression of the workers' movement and the growth of the industrial economy launched a period of increasing wealth and a boom in the stock market. It is brilliantly portrayed by Narcís Oller in his novel *La febre d'or* (*Gold Fever*, 1890–2). Its opening is Dickensian. The rushing feet up and down the stairs of Barcelona's stock exchanges, the shouts that mark the rise and fall of share prices and the stampedes that follow capture the atmosphere of the era. The book follows the rise and rise and subsequent fall of Gil Foix, share dealer and speculator, and of those who both depend on and exploit him. It is, as we might expect, a tale of greed overwhelming reason and logic at a time when – as with so many economic bubbles – it can seem that prices and profits can only rise forever.

Foix is a character we might recognise from other novels of the period. The child of an ordinary family – his father was a carpenter – from the little town of Vilaniu, he travelled to Havana in search of the fortune that others had found there. He returned no wealthier, however, but a small inheritance allowed him to move to Barcelona and to embark on a career in the stock exchange. From the outset he is assailed by less successful relatives from his hometown, sycophants looking for a share in his good fortune and, more importantly perhaps, in the status that money brings. Gil seems cautious at first, encouraged by his wife Catalina, who is deeply suspicious of the fawning cousins and counsels him against parting with his money too easily. Nonetheless, she is persuaded to move to Carrer Ample near the harbour, where some of the city's hereditary rich still live.

Everyone was mentioning unfamiliar names of people who had come from nowhere and acquired the status of potentates; they spent more on luxuries now than the nobility, the bankers and the old merchants. The theatres, always full, were dazzling. The ironmongers' and joiners' shops were disappearing to give way to jewellers and expensive furniture stores. The confectioners, milliners, bakeries and luxury restaurants were multiplying as if by magic.

Gil's daughter Delfina is scornful of her father's ignorance of protocol, in other words of his status as one of the nouveaux riches, and it is her vision that seems to inform the description of what is intended as an elegant dinner to mark their new and improved circumstances. It is comic, but cruel – the soup proves too thick, the wine ill chosen, the oysters hard to manage, and the whole event descends into chaos. Nonetheless, business is going well for Foix. Yet, 'Gil Foix wasn't content with money; he wanted social status and fame. The financial world and building a railway to Vilaniu could give him both.'

5 *Narcís Oller, author of* Gold Fever

The cast of characters is a kind of soap opera of the rising Barcelona bourgeoisie, who endlessly gossip about one another's dubious social backgrounds, the elegant wealthy sisters who speak Castilian mixed with French with hauteur, the ambitious and manipulative country cousins who will eventually succumb to their own greed, the officials and politicians who rush to congratulate the nouveau riche for whom they feel only contempt. Foix himself is a comic figure in some ways but also a credible representative of the delusions of the stock market booms and of the contradictions of a provincial middle class that has gravitated to Barcelona and then discovered other metropolises beyond – Paris and London. But Foix is a speculator not an industrialist like Agustí's heroes – and, as every generation would soon discover, the stock exchange and the banks are built on sand. As a portrait of an ostentatious and over-confident middle class, the book is telling.

When, as seemed inevitable, the dreams of avarice bring disaster, the words of Bernat, Foix's brother, who rises above the world of easy money, are a kind of final judgement on Foix and his ilk: 'You will see that a gambler's money doesn't last, and that those who enter the stock exchange are getting on a paper balloon. It will rise into the air to show them wonderful views [. . .] Then it will suddenly catch fire and [. . .] bang! they will hit the ground, no bones, no clothes [. . .] nothing.'

In the event, the boom was halted by end of the 1870s, when the phylloxera that had devastated the French wine crop, allowing a brief bonanza for the Catalan wine-growers, crossed the Pyrenees and wreaked havoc in the Catalan vineyards, forcing the planting of a new cross-bred grape variety. This was, nonetheless, a Barcelona built in the spirit of a confident modernity. The streets that Oller describes were walkways for the beneficiaries of prosperity.

Ignacio Agustí's *Mariona Rebull*, mentioned earlier, also narrates the rise of a new industrial bourgeoisie, through the story of Mariona, a young woman born into the more traditional rural nobility, and Joaquín Rius, the scion of the Rius family, whose history is itself the story of the emergence of industrial Barcelona.

The older Joaquín had worked in his father's modest herbalist's shop, but with ambitions far beyond this small family business. Announcing to his wife that he was leaving for Cuba, and that 'he would return a rich man', he was away for nearly ten years. When he returned, with two bottles of French champagne and a Cuban connection, he bought several plots of land and moved quickly into industrial production:

> The Rius family were by then one of the wealthiest families in the city. Recently returned from America, where he had travelled with only what he was wearing, the father had placed some looms in the back room of a shop he had opened a few months earlier. It prospered rapidly. In ten years he was rumoured to have three sites in various parts of the city, on one of which he was building an apartment block.

He is soon the owner of half a dozen looms, but the family's lifestyle changes little. He rises precisely at six and his son Joaquín attends the expensive private Jesuit school. Once he graduates, Joaquín expresses little interest in the aristocratic habits of his schoolfriend Ernesto Villar. Instead, he sees in his own face 'the inexorable traces and the undeniable expression of the merchant', and he elects to join his father at the factory. Together father and son follow the same regular pattern, leaving their home at six and devoting their day to production. The two travel to London, and on his return Joaquin insists that the family move to a more elegant and more suitable apartment, one more appropriate for their well-endowed circumstances. At 25, Joaquín looks and acts like a 40-year-old, deciding that a wife is an essential accoutrement for a wealthy businessman.

The woman he chooses, in a calculated way, is Mariona, the young daughter of an old family of jewellers. Her father is a craftsman with a deep distrust for the money-making, materialistic

Riuses, and his daughter is a romantic with little interest in the trappings of wealth, easily seduced by Joaquín's dandified classmate Ernesto Villar, who lives a dissolute life with family money. At the Universal Exposition of 1888, the Riuses are received by the Queen, raising their social status considerably, but Mariona rejects Joaquín's proposal. The suave and confident Villar is always in the background, and it will emerge that he is the reason for Mariona's reluctance to marry. In a sense a central theme of the novel is the tension between romantic love and a rational materialism. Joaquín's decision to overcome his anger and propose to her for a second time is motivated more by a sense of what a man in his position ought to do than by any impulsive passion. As she says to him in a later dialogue, when they are married and have a child, 'I am not another piece of machinery in your factory. For you,' she says, 'everything is calculation and appearance, obligation and the respect of other men.' Later, when he returns to the plant, he smells the cotton and hears the sound of the loom and is filled with 'a vague, insistent, liberating sense of calm'. His feelings are merely conventions; his sense of himself comes from the clacking of the looms.

Like all those of his class, he is pointedly aware of the rising tensions in the street. 'There's no room in my factory for idleness or revolution,' he declares. And he pays little attention to the anonymous threatening letters that warn that he will suffer the same fate as the businessman Llopis, killed by an anarchist in the street. Agustí's novel is a combination of a slightly anachronistic realism and a melodrama of love and jealousy. The mix itself reflects the tensions in the society he is depicting. Mariona's family seat is in a rural Cataluña of deferential peasants, loyal servants and a grumpy local priest; it is her heritage and family name that makes her such a perfect match. When Joaquín insists on moving to more luxurious accommodation in the city centre, she is ill at ease. 'Somehow it felt like an invented place. Mariona missed the stained-glass windows with their fans, the pictures marked with age – in a word a tradition, an atmosphere, that she couldn't quite define.'

Gold Fever and *Mariona Rebull* are novels which – as Camilo Jose Cela says of Oller's work – 'see themselves as history': history as the encounter between individual ambition and the movements of social and technological forces. And two events, portrayed in different ways in the novels, mark the points of dramatic transition, in psychological as well as material terms. The 1888 Universal Exposition was a public display of confidence by a city and its rising bourgeois class. The events at the iconic Liceu theatre in 1893, as described earlier, were the most shocking expression of the tensions simmering just beneath the surface, which Joaquín Rius had so obviously, and tragically, dismissed.

The Universal Exposition of 1888

The city was on holiday. The Queen Mother and her distinguished son Alfonso XIII, the young King, together with the princesses and their court, had come from Madrid to open the Universal Exposition. The city streets filled with multicoloured uniforms, with foreigners, and visitors. You should have seen the exhibition grounds! Wide avenues had been opened, all wonderfully laid with sand; beautiful palaces where you could sip a sweet lemonade or a bright blue *granizado*. Great hotels had been built, one of them – the International – in just 42 days, and their rooms occupied by curious and motley population that had come from Paris, Vienna, London – from Europe! Crowds of sailors from many nations gave the city an intoxicating touch of colour [. . .] The ships of the French, English, Dutch and American fleet were anchored outside the port and people from every social class crowded on to the 'golondrina' pleasure boats and sailed for an hour through the horrors of seasickness just to see the colossal bellies of the ships arriving laden with pennants. At night there were *serenatas*, dances, magic shows and cockfights in the exhibition grounds, and lectures, concerts and fraternal events between nations.

This is Ignacio Agustí's description, in *Mariona Rebull,* of the Barcelona Universal Exposition of 1888, a celebration of modernity and technological progress that followed similar events in Paris and Vienna in previous years. Its impact on the Barcelona of the time is reflected in all the literature of or about the period. Clearly it was seen not only as an important event in itself, but also as a confirmation of Barcelona's membership of a modernising Europe, a way of asserting its difference from Madrid and perhaps its distance from the rest of Spain. The city has held such events at regular intervals since then, as we shall see, and each has heralded a transformation of the city as well as an affirmation of its cultural traditions, its language and its distinction.

Cristina and Eduardo Mendoza have a rather different view of the exhibition. 'It was nothing special,' they say, in their book *Barcelona moderniste* (2003). 'It was like the coming-out party for the ugly daughter of a poor family.' It is perhaps a rather harsh judgement, but for all its rapid economic development Barcelona could not compete technologically with London or Paris.

Yet Barcelona was the only city in the Spanish state that could put on such an exhibition, even though it was nearly crippled by the expense. Madrid was still an administrative centre proud of its *castizo* (authentically Spanish) character, but it remained quite provincial, as the novels of Benito Pérez Galdós show. Barcelona's selection for the exhibition met with general approval in Madrid, for the same reasons, and the Queen's attendance at the exhibition's opening marked a kind of political reconciliation between the constitutional monarchy and a Cataluña politically conservative but still fiercely proud of its cultural and linguistic traditions.

It seemed symbolically fitting that the main site of the exhibition should be the Ciutadella, now demolished and transformed into a public park. And for once the cannons fired from Montjuich were not directed at an insurrectionary city but in celebration of the exhibition's inauguration on 20 May 1888. It would remain open until December and receive 2 million visitors. It also provided employment and an enormous boost for a troubled construction industry. Many of those who came to the city as temporary workers remained, and by 1900 the city's population had doubled in less than 20 years. The Hotel Internacional, with its 2,000 rooms, was reputed to have been built in somewhere between 48 and 62 days; it stood on the Paseo Colón, within sight of both the main exhibition buildings and the monument to Columbus at the foot of the Ramblas, which the writer Manuel Vázquez Montalbán would later describe as a 'giant paperweight' and Andre Pierre de Mandiargues as an enormous phallic symbol.

Of the exhibition buildings themselves, all that remain today are the Arc de Trionf, the original entrance, the Castell de les Tres Dracs (Three Dragons Castle), once the restaurant and now the Zoology Museum, and part of the Machine Gallery which is incorporated into the Barcelona Zoo that occupies much of the original site. In the park, the extraordinary Gran Cascada fountain falls over statuary and artificial nature overlooked by a great arch and four golden horses, an eclectic celebration of a Neoclassicism – *noucentrisme* – that would become an important alternative to the Renaixença (Renaissance). The exhibition was a milestone, at least in the internal life of the city. Indeed, the decision to hold it fell to one man, Barcelona's mayor Rius y Tallet, who famously slammed down his fist in the middle of a council meeting dominated by sceptics and swore dramatically, silencing his opponents.

Like most events of the kind, then and since, the cost of the exhibition inevitably flew out of control, the ambitions far outrunning the resources. As is so often the case, and would be again in the experience of many cities, such events are rarely economically viable – their purposes are of a different order, about prestige and status. The Exposition was approved in a moment of economic crisis, the end of the gold fever that had enriched some, impoverished many, and favoured only the bankers and insurance companies. The exhibition in that sense was a rescue operation. As Eduardo Mendoza describes it in his wonderful novel *City of Marvels* (1989):

People everywhere in Barcelona were hospitable to the visitors, even when it meant putting up with considerable trouble and inconvenience – for which they received no thanks, as is usually the case under such circumstances. Generally, the visitors assumed a haughty air, fussed at the least thing and remarked as they toured 'How disgusting, what a place, what inane people.' They believed that to show disdain was to show good breeding [. . .] The World's Fair remained open until December 9 1888. It had lasted 245 days and had been visited by over two million peoples. The costs totalled 5,684,657 pesetas. Some of the buildings could be used for other purposes, but the debt incurred was enormous and weighed on the Barcelona City Council for many years thereafter. The memory of those days of splendour also lingered on and the notion that Barcelona, if it chose to, could once again become a cosmopolitan city.

The City of Marvels

As the last decade of the nineteenth century began, the economic crisis had not been overcome. One effect of the Universal Exposition had been to attract foreign companies and commerce to the expanding areas of the city and especially to the Eixample's Rambla de Cataluña and the Paseo de Gracia, the Champs Elysées of this aspiring second Paris. The effect was to put a number of local enterprises out of business. Other sectors (but not the wily Onofre Bouvila of Mendoza's *City of Marvels*) were the victims of the wild speculation that preceded and accompanied the exhibition, at least those who had survived the collapse of the previous decade's gold fever. Thousands of workers lost their jobs as the Madrid government withdrew the protectionist measures that had always given Catalan industry a margin of safety. One result was the deepening of the social crisis. It had two expressions. The first was the rise of anarchist influence in the mass trade unions that were now forming in the city and launching strikes and street actions. The other manifestation was what was called 'physical force anarchism', the use of violent assaults on powerful people, at public events and against public institutions. The thinking behind these actions was never entirely clear, even when they were often reactions to specific situations.

The bombing of the Liceu theatre at the start of the 1893 season shook the city to its core. As mentioned earlier, it was in fact a retaliation for the execution of another anarchist, Paulino Pallas, who had thrown a bomb at Captain General Martínez Campos weeks earlier, wounding the general and killing one civil guard.

The violence was a response to a rapidly deteriorating situation. The expanded working population, now well over 550,000 in number, lived in dark, crowded rooms with no facilities or support, often sharing space with their animals, as Mendoza describes it:

> The reality had not changed; with walls or without them, the city remained just as cramped. People lived out their lives in tiny, squalid rooms, in evil-smelling and indecent promiscuity. With the city walls gone, the valley that swept out to the foothills of the Sierra de Collserola was in full view all day, so that the overcrowding became even more glaring. Damnation, the citizens would say, all that empty land and here we are stuck like rats in holes. Is it fair that we should be worse off than those lettuces?

The extension of the Eixample continued after the exhibition, but with no regard at all to Cerdà's original plans. In a frenzy of speculation, the original plans and promises were thrust aside, the living spaces made ever smaller, the original aspiration to squares and parks forgotten. In *City of Marvels,* Mendoza is withering in his description of how the area was built. And his central character, Onofre, is the embodiment of the gangster capitalist, the heartless speculator, the kind of man who has grown rich not simply by cheating others, but by building on their greed and their yearning for power. The literature of late nineteenth-century Barcelona is full of similar characters, though Mendoza's Onofre and Oller's financier Gil Foix are perhaps the most complex representations.

In 1895, the second war of liberation was launched in Spain's only remaining Latin American colony, Cuba, the final remnant of its empire. It was led by the poet and political leader José Martí, albeit briefly – he was killed in the first battle of the war. In the three years of warfare before Cuba finally became independent, Spain gained a reputation for ruthless and brutal repression. The Spanish army was commanded by a Catalan, Weyler, whose name is linked to the first concentration camps, which he established on the island. The Cuban nationalists were fierce and determined adversaries, but it was cholera and yellow fever that wreaked the greatest havoc among Spanish troops.

The Catalan middle classes were driven further into the arms of Madrid by the growing social discontent, and its increasingly threatening character. It was, after all, the young men of the poor districts – the same people who had marched and demonstrated and organised strikes and protests – who were now force-marched down to the port of Barcelona to board the troop ships that would take them, in their hundreds and thousands, to fight a colonial war under appalling conditions. By 1898, Spain was no longer a colonial power – it had lost Cuba and the Philippines, and Sidi Ifni, Spanish Morocco, was its single remaining colonial outpost. Those troops who limped home – often mutilated and ravaged by disease – left hundreds of thousands of dead behind them. And at home they were received as cowards and traitors rather than heroes, as is always the case with defeated armies.

The demoralisation that followed Spain's final demise as an imperial power was expressed by writers across the country, among them the great poet Antonio Machado, who described a suit of armour rusting on the plains of Castile as a suitable metaphor for post-1898 Spain. In Barcelona, specifically, the returning wounded were received with rage and mourning. The anger at the growing gulf between the ostentatious prosperity of some and the unrelieved poverty of the majority found expression in the growth of anarchism in the city.

The beneficiaries of Barcelona's prosperity found common cause with the government in Madrid. Prime Minister Cánovas had been their reliable ally, and his death served to reinforce their fear of the masses, and their distance from Catalan nationalism. The very wealthy were now flattered with aristocratic titles endowed by Madrid, and they began to use Castilian expressions and fashions. Oller illustrates it very wittily in *Gold Fever* when the young daughter of the ambitious financier Gil Foix insists on calling him 'Papá', with the accent on the final 'a'. In Catalan it is not stressed – it is simply 'Papa'.

Barcelona was changing, its population of workers grew as migrants from Andalucia and Murcia came to the city in search of work – and with none of the allegiances that a previous generation of largely Catalan-speaking migrants had maintained. It was especially among these new migrants that anarchism found fertile soil in the dark cellars of the Raval. It was their sons who failed to return from the colonial wars, after all. There was a powerful reaction among the middle classes too to the disaster of 1898. Calpena reports on a concert by a visiting French orchestra in 1899 who were booed when they played the Spanish national anthem but cheered to the rooftops for their rendition of 'La Marseillaise'. The Catalan middle class felt aggrieved that they were asked to pay a higher proportion of tax towards the costs of war precisely because industry paid a higher rate than property. In October 1898 there was a strike in the retail sector, which was ended by the declaration of a state of emergency.

Despite the crisis, however, the turn of the century saw growing prosperity, the continuing expansion of the Eixample, a culture of consumption and luxury, the first cinemas. While the living standards of the poor remained unchanged, the life of a prosperous bourgeois was as rich in consumer goods as any in Europe. Its confidence found expression in a new school of art and architecture, Modernisme, in its grand houses along the Paseo de Gracia in particular.

The life story of Onofre Bouvila, the central figure of Mendoza's *City of Marvels*, parallels the life of the city between the Universal Expositions of 1888 and 1929. One among many migrants from rural Catalonia, Onofre's father was one of those who sought his fortune in Cuba and (apparently) grew rich there.

Onofre arrives in Barcelona in 1887, just a year before the exhibition. He is possibly 13 years old, and penniless: 'Now Barcelona, like the female of a strange species that has just given birth to numerous offspring, lay exhausted from loss of blood; stinking streams flowed from the drains, foul smells made the air in streets and houses unbreathable. The population was suffering from weariness and pessimism.'

Above all, Onofre is an individual survivor, owing no allegiances and pursuing only his own benefit; he is a creature of this new, unforgiving, capitalist universe. And in the end he becomes its controller. Unburdened by scruples, Onofre moves with the tides of change. He deploys the instruments, human and explosive, of a criminal underworld to impose his own will through those he controls, like Don Braulio, his erstwhile host at the boarding house where he first arrived, who travels the lower depths in women's clothing on Onofre's behalf. But Onofre's wealth does not admit him to the circles of the old and new nobility who happily accept his contributions but never his presence. When the Czarina of Russia visits Barcelona, a delegation of important local people request finance from him to pay for the visit and ensure it is conducted with appropriate style. On the day of the grand banquet, Onofre is denied a place at high table, and is seated – as it turns out – beside Rasputin.

As he moves from organised crime to dealing in arms and later into a nascent film industry, Onofre shows his 'limitless confidence in his capacity to survive any and every eventuality'. When he is asked how that is so, his reply is to describe himself as 'a flaw in the system'. Yet the novel shows him as a man wholly in tune with the nature and the progress of this system he has entered and come to dominate. From time to time he experiences love but cannot cope with its denial. His first (and later) love – Delfina, daughter of the boarding house owner – introduces him to anarchism and gives him his first job distributing leaflets outside the 1888 Exposition site. He soon abandons that for selling hair restorer in the street. Later the crooked lawyer Don Humberto refuses Onofre his daughter's hand – he is hardly a suitable match for a noble family! As ever, Onofre gets his way. His final love affair is with the daughter of another eccentric, the inventor Belltall, who will be indirectly responsible for the novel's glorious ending – which I shall not reveal.

In these three fine novels, *Mariona Rebull, Gold Fever* and *The City of Marvels*, Barcelona becomes much more than a mere setting. It is, in each case, an actor and a presence, influencing and shaping the characters. In Barcelona's theatres, the most successful play was Angel Guimera's *Terra Baixa* (*Low Country*, 1897). Its theme is the conflict between a world of money and ambition, symbolised by the landowner Don Sebastian, and the traditional world of the peasants in the highlands. Sebastian's abuse of Marta and his entrapment of her father, forcing him to allow it, makes her a tragic heroine. Sebastian obliges her to marry the naive shepherd Manolic, who lives in the high mountains, to cover himself. In the end, authenticity and honour survive in the ancient and traditional communities of the hills, and Manolic proves to himself and to Marta that he is a person of far greater moral worth than the corrupt and unscrupulous Sebastian. The play has remained part of the Catalan repertoire and has been filmed several times, both within Cataluña and beyond. Leni Riefenstahl, Hitler's favourite director, made a film based on it – echoing the idea of the high mountains as a representation of a pure and uncorrupted nature.

# 4

AT THE SIGN OF
FOUR CATS

That afternoon, after closing the shop, my father suggested that we stroll along to the Els Quatre Gats, a café on Calle Montsió, where Barceló and his bibliophile knights of the round table gathered to discuss the finer points of decadent poets, dead languages, and neglected, moth-ridden masterpieces.

El Quatre Gats was just a five-minute walk from our house and one of my favourite haunts. My parents had met there in 1932, and I attributed my one-way ticket into this world to the old café's charms. Stone dragons guarded a lamp-lit façade. Inside, voices seemed to echo with shadows of other times. Accountants, dreamers and would-be geniuses shared tables with the spectres of Pablo Picasso, Isaac Albéniz, Federico García Lorca and Salvador Dalí. There any poor devil could pass for a historical figure for the price of a small coffee.

The café described in Carlos Ruiz Zafón's *The Shadow of the Wind*, where Daniel's parents first met, still draws in visitors of every kind – no doubt still including some accountants and some dreamers. It was opened over a century ago, in 1897, and with interruptions has remained in the Calle Montsió ever since. It won its reputation in the six years between 1897 and 1903, when it was opened by Pere Romeu together with the artists Ramon Casas and Santiago Ruisiñol, the leading lights of Barcelona's Modernisme circle. The bar was dominated by Casas's painting of himself and Romeu riding a tandem, to symbolise their Bohemianism and modernity. The image still dominates the café, whose name 'Quatre Gats', literally 'Four Cats', is probably best equated to the English phrase 'Three Men and a Dog'.

Casas and Ruisiñol were both sons of wealthy families, which enabled them to spend time living in Paris absorbing the lessons of French Impressionism and savouring the delights of Montmartre. When they returned, Ruisiñol's house in the fashionable resort of Sitges, near Barcelona, Cau Ferrat, became a focus of the Modernisme movement, displaying paintings by themselves as well as less internationally known artists such as Isidro Nonell and Joaquín Mir. Regular concerts there included performances by avant-garde composers like César Franck and Claude Débussy, Manuel de Falla and Erik Satie, while the bourgeoisie of the city favoured Wagner, having abandoned its previous allegiance to Italian opera. As Colm Tóibín puts it, in his *Homage to Barcelona*:

> Neither Casas nor Ruisiñol became an Impressionist; their work is closer to Whistler than Renoir. Their landscapes are softly lit, their gardens are ordered and picturesque, the faces of the women they painted are tender. What they brought home with them from Paris, besides a style of painting which emphasised light and mood, was a sense of the cosmopolitan world beyond the Pyrenees. They became leaders, trend-setters.

As we have seen, they lived in a period of social conflict and an emerging anarchism. Yet the leading artistic radicals often seemed distant from that reality. However, in three paintings Ramon Casas marked key moments in Barcelona's social confrontations. *Garrotte vil* (1893) imagines the execution by garote outside the walls of Montjuich Castle of Santiago Salvador, who threw the bomb in the Liceu. *Corpus* (1896) depicts the bomb thrown at Martínez Campos during the Corpus procession, now widely assumed to have been the action of an agent provocateur, with the aim of legitimising the severe repression that followed. *La carga* (*The Charge*, 1899) shows a mounted civil guard attacking a worker with his sabre. Ruisiñol, like Nonell and Picasso, also painted occasional portraits of the poor, such as his *Before the Morphine* of 1894.

These were indications of the discontent that would explode in the Semana Trágica, the Tragic Week, of 1909. Yet by the turn of the century the radical impulses of some of the Modernistas had been tamed. Casas, now a highly fashionable and sought-after figure, was designing posters and publicity for large commercial firms such as Anís del Mono; some writers, like Ramon Casellas, were already moving towards a conservative position. Narcís Oller's work became more focused on his growing interest in psychology and he spent more time now on theatre and translation than on novels.

Ruisiñol was both artist and writer, his plays – largely satirical – were regularly presented in Barcelona's theatres, and his columns appeared in several local newspapers. In Joan Fuster's *Literatura catalane contemporanea* (1972) he summed up the Modernisme creed:

> This movement that has burst forth has mysticism, insofar as it is suffering and vision; anarchism insofar as it is improbable fantasy; symbolism insofar as it takes us far from home; idealistic revolution in its lack of faith in the practices of men; it has everything that is implied in dreaming, alone, without interference from the wealthy or the impoverished or the art bourgeois who do not tremble when they are face to face with a sunset, a weeping woman, or a passing cloud tinged with red or a rising dawn.

Nonell, the youngest of the Quatre Gats circle, by contrast, painted the inmates of a hospital for the mentally ill in graphic and powerful terms, before turning to the population of the Raval. Picasso, too, still not yet 20, exhibited his drawings of the inhabitants of the poor districts at the café in 1900. Some of them would inhabit the paintings of his early Blue Period, which began while he was still living in the city and attending the Quatre Gats gatherings. There is, though, no record of any active engagement by the Bohemians with the anarchist groups organising the working people of the city. And the anarchists in their turn had little time for the painters. It would seem rather, as Robert Hughes suggests, that these young artists felt a more general but abstract sympathy for the dispossessed who were at times the subjects of their work.

Ruisiñol was a less significant artist than Casas, but his activities spread more widely. He was an essayist, an artistic entrepreneur, a regular columnist in the press, and a playwright. His most successful play was *L'auca del senyor Esteve*, which began life as a book with illustrations by Casas, published in 1907. The *auca* was a traditional Catalan art form in which stories were told in a series of images, each with an accompanying couplet. Ruisiñol's work is in some senses a satire on the emerging commercial bourgeoisie.

The Esteve of the title runs the family hosiery and linen business, La Principal, in the La Ribera district, now the centre of a burgeoning commercial sector. The book begins on the day of the birth of Mr Esteve's son, Estevet.

> It could not have been a less cheerful day for a birth, but Señor Ramon Esteve did not have time for the luxury of sadness. With one ear listening to the customers' requests, and another to the upper floor in case he was needed, his mind leapt back and forth from his wife's bed to the scales downstairs. What was happening in the bedroom was serious – he was becoming a father – but what was happening in the shop was just as serious; it was business.

Growing up, Estevet seems ideally suited to his future role.

> His early inclinations and interests were limited to the shop. He would spend hours tying and untying string, as if he wanted

to count the threads, or already knew how important weights and measures would be. And he always returned things to their proper place, never making a mistake. With a few dozen buttons, piling them up, sorting them out, he could play for a whole afternoon. And if he lost one he would be moody. Days would pass as he arranged empty boxes, as if he already had the instincts of a collector.

When the grown-up Estevet, now 30, marries and has a son, Ramonet, the assumption is that he will continue the business, and the line. But Ramonet has a secret passion. While he says nothing to his parents, he regularly disappears to the Llotja after work. His parents clearly do not understand that it is not only a commercial exchange, but also the location of the School of Art; not even their son's peculiar long-haired friends help them to see

6 *Ramon Casas's famous 1901 painting* Garrote vil, *portraying an execution*

what is happening. But Ramonet loyally accepts his role in the shop, growing moodier and sadder as time passes.

The climax (if that is the right word for such an ordered and calculated universe) of the story, however, comes when Estevet invites his wife, his son and his daughter-in-law to the theatre, to see a play entitled *The Good People*, or perhaps *Respectable People*. The first act, in which the main character, Mr Batista, a pawnbroker, occupies the stage, reassures Estevet.

> The things Batista said about commerce, about accounts and how to keep them, seemed well argued, he felt, and his ambition to make money honourably was the most natural thing in the world. He had raised the profile of the business by saving, and anyone who does that will always reach the highest levels and be able to face and overcome the most difficult circumstances.

The second act, however, introduced the son, whose ambition was to become a painter, much to Estevet's disgust. His loud critical comments provoke angry calls from other audience members for him to be silent. After the interval, Batista has become a banker, suffering from gout and badly mistreating his wife. That is of little significance to Estevet, compared with his financial success. In a moment of elderly weakness, the banker recants and gives his money away, but then changes his mind and recovers it and puts it back in the safe, to Estevet's relief.

Yet on his own deathbed, Estevet does relent and, calling his son to him, says, 'You will be a sculptor. I have always seen you at the counter, but you did it for me and I'm grateful. Remember I, who never was anyone in the world, made this money so that you could do what you wanted. See it as a way of fertilising the soil so that the plant can grow.'

The story of the Esteves is, inescapably, contemptuous of the merchant class, anti-bourgeois from the rather aristocratic position that Ruisiñol occupied, and which allowed him the luxury of scorning the accumulation of capital. It is revealing of the contradiction at Modernisme's heart: it was artistically revolutionary but in many cases, like Ruisiñol, socially conservative.

A Backward Glance

Ruisiñol, like most of his contemporaries, wrote almost entirely in Catalan. In that sense they were the heirs of an earlier artistic movement centred on the revival of Catalan culture launched by Carles Aribau's poem 'La Patria' ('Homeland'), published in 1833. It is ironic, considering its enormous impact, that this was the only poem that Aribau ever wrote in Catalan. He moved on to become a civil servant in Madrid and gave up writing altogether.

Cataluña did not have a Romantic movement as such, but the burgeoning Catalan middle class rediscovered its identity in the landscape and the history of a Catalan people whose history remained largely unrecognised for nearly a century. Aribau captured both the idealised landscape and the nostalgia that informed this early literary nationalism:

> Goodbye, my hills, goodbye forever,
> You rugged mountains that, in my homeland,
> Stood out against the clouds and sky
> In your eternal, restful blue.
> Goodbye old Montseny, who from your mountain palace
> Like a vigilant guardian, covered in mist and snow,
> Look down through a gap on the tomb of the Jew
> And the Mallorcan ship on the great open sea.

A later verse provides the key to the poem's success.

> My first infant cry was in Catalan
> When I sucked milk from my mother's sweet breast

Every day I prayed to God in Catalan
And every night sang Catalan songs in my dreams
When I am alone, I speak to my soul
In Catalan, the only language that it knows,
And then no lies are spoken, it cannot lie
And the words arise from my very heart.

A few years later, the writer and poet Joaquim Rubio i Ors published a collection of his own writings in Catalan, *Lo gayter de Llobregat* (*The Piper of Llobregat*, 1841), whose introduction would become a kind of manifesto for the new art in a newly self-aware cultural nation. It was a plea for the recovery of 'our ancient and melodious language', the language of the troubadours of Languedoc, popular poets of the medieval world; this would be Cataluña's own Renaissance – La Renaixença. The historical foundation for this new movement lay in Capmany's *Historical Memoirs*, a work of the Enlightenment as significant in the Catalan context as the *Encyclopédie* itself. The irony, of course, was that this renaissance and affirmation of the Catalan past was written in Castilian Spanish, evidence in itself of how far that past and its language had been denied any cultural or intellectual stature.

Against that background Rubio i Ors's proposal was genuinely radical, and his call for a revival of the Jocs Florals – the Floral Games of medieval times at which poets and singers could compete in Catalan – was revealing, but not only of the importance of Catalan itself. The backward glance, the search for cultural legitimacy in a past idealised and affirmed in its continuity with the present, were echoes of European Romantic nationalism. It was interesting, for example, that Aribau had in his youth edited a newspaper called *El Europeo* (*The European*).

The first Jocs Florals were organised 18 years later, in 1859. Despite their celebration of rural folklore and the humble peasant (*pagès*) as the incarnation of an authentic Cataluña, the portraits of the first and subsequent games leave little doubt that they were a very bourgeois affair, the self-affirmation of the rising Catalan middle class. Significantly, the first games were held in the great hall of the Consell de Cent, the Council of One Hundred that had governed medieval Barcelona. The Renaixença set that past in a continuum towards a future in which Catalan would recover its rightful place at the heart of culture and where a middle class without a state could assert its nationhood – and most importantly its modernity. In this sense, as Michael Eaude reminds us in *Barcelona*, it was: 'unlike Basque nationalism [. . .] which was originally a reaction against modernity, a flight back to rural values, Barcelona's famous architects and their patrons were also on the whole conservative, but they were urban people, forward-looking in their outlook and European in their cultural desires.'

At this early stage, however, the Renaixença remained cautious. The leading figures in the movement, such as Aribau and Milà i Fontanals, the scholar and collector of the poetic traditions, were personally conservative, but they were at the same time Europeans, who saw Paris as their cultural Mecca. In general, the contributions to the Jocs Florals were not of any great aesthetic merit. They tended to be patriotic and sentimental epics, at least at first. The finest expressions of the Renaixença would come a little later with the rise of Anselm Clavé's choral movement, and the publication of Jacint Verdaguer's epic *L'Atlàntida* (*Atlantis*), which won the Jocs Florals in 1877.

In *Ghosts of Spain*, Giles Tremlett describes Verdaguer as 'the towering figure of a prolonged Renaissance – the *Renaixença* – whose lengthy Catalan-language epics to his homeland had made him a kind of Catalan Tennyson'. It is not entirely clear whether Tremlett means that as a compliment. But within Cataluña Verdaguer's status as a national poet is undeniable, despite his later descent into madness, or at the very least eccentricity. His writing elevated Catalan to a literary language worthy of the name, rich and expansive. Born in 1845 to a humble working family in the region of Vic, the heartland of Catalan, Verdaguer was ordained a priest at the age of 25. He participated in the Jocs Florals of 1865 and was then employed as a shipboard chaplain by the Trasatlántica, the shipping company owned and run by one of the wealthiest and most powerful of the *indianos*, Antonio López, later Marqués de Comillas. In 1870, the López family had taken over the huge eighteenth-century Palau Mojá, at the corner of the Ramblas and Carrer Puertaferrisa. Although, like most of the *indianos*, López had made his initial fortune as a slave trader in Cuba, and later added greater wealth through his trading and banking interests, he and his son Claudio were given to charitable works. Hence the appointment of the deeply religious Verdaguer to the role of 'alms chaplain', disbursing charity among the poor. By then Verdaguer was a prominent and respected literary figure, and he was given accommodation within the palace. His epic poem *L'Atlàntida* had won the attention of the city's cultural elite, and in 1878 he was called to Rome, where he discussed his work with the Pope. In 1883 100,000 copies of his 'Oda a Barcelona' ('Ode to Barcelona') were printed and distributed by Barcelona's City Council. Three years later he was given the accolade 'Poet of Cataluña' by the Bishop of Ripoll.

L'Atlàntida was written during his two years of voyages between Cataluña and Cuba aboard the ships of the Transatlántica. It is built around the epic journey of a Genoese sailor, who we later discover is Columbus. Shipwrecked, the navigator lands on an island occupied by an old hermit who narrates the poem and its story of a mythic world populated by Greek heroes and once occupied by the legendary city of Atlantis. It describes Hercules' Atlantic journeys, his encounters with and defeat of the dragon guarding the golden apples, and finally his return to Cataluña. It is a rich, expansive and dramatic work which places Cataluña in continuity with an ancient, mythic world. But most importantly, it is an epic in high literary Catalan. Its confident affirmation of a classical Catalan was perhaps its most important contribution.

Verdaguer continued to live in the palace on the Ramblas but apparently took his charitable work too seriously, bringing poor families into the Palau Mojá and distributing the López's largesse throughout the Raval. After his acclamation as a national poet, Verdaguer seemed to undergo a personal crisis which led him into a more manic phase. Queues of supplicants formed in the Ramblas, and Verdaguer responded to them all. Prelates were called in to restore his equilibrium, while on the other hand a local false mystic used him in a series of exorcisms. Eventually, denied the right to say Mass, he was exiled from Barcelona; but he returned and wrote a series of fairly unhinged articles defending himself and claiming he was the subject of persecution. His erstwhile hosts threw him out and he moved in with one of the families he had supported, until finding refuge in the Barcelona suburb of Vallvidrera, in Villa Joanna, a country mansion which is now a heritage site. He died there on 10 June 1902.

Verdaguer was a key figure in a first phase of a Catalan revival, his work an affirmation of the richness of Catalan language and a celebration of its continuity through time with its origins in a mystical, mythic past. The Renaixença was only one aspect of the Catalan revival. The other was the emergence of a modern, industrial city and the birth within it of a radical workers' movement. That contrast would define the city, in multiple and contradictory ways, as it entered the era of modernity. Its Modernisme, however, contained both elements. And the greatest exponent of Modernisme, Antoni Gaudí, was far closer to Verdaguer than to the artists and writers who gathered at Ruisiñol's house in Sitges or attended the early meetings at the Quatre Gats.

Looking for Gaudí

The Modernisme to which Gaudí belonged was hostile to the Sitges circle and its leaders, and critical of the Bohemian morality they so ostentatiously represented. It was principally a movement in architecture and the visual arts. Its major literary figure was the poet Joan Maragall, who shared with Gaudí a deep religious conviction.

Maragall's first book of poetry was published in 1895, when he was 35 years old; by then he had participated in several of the events at Sitges organised by the Ruisiñol/Casas circle, and identified with the Modernistas. But he did not share their Bohemianism. The child of a wealthy family, he was a lawyer, a journalist with the *Diario de Barcelona* and, to all appearances, a respectable family man (he and his English wife had 13 children). Yet he is widely seen as the most important Modernista writer, evidence of the fact that what the Modernistas shared in their vision of art did not imply that they had values in common. Maragall was, in a clear sense, a follower of the Romantics in his work, and he agreed with Shelley's view of poetry's ethical obligations, its role as a kind of moral compass in society.

In one sense, that set the poet apart, since his independence was the essence of his vision, but it did not mean that he shared the idea of the poet as outsider, as a moral outlaw, that others in the Modernista movement did. In the mid-1890s he expressed his outrage at the 'decadence' of the Modernista circles. His early work picked up on the Catalanist themes of the Renaixença, but his celebrations of Catalan culture (like his poem on the *sardana*, the national dance) are less sentimental than an earlier generation's. His defence of Catalan as a language best suited to the increasingly spiritual, religious concerns of his writing sat alongside the Castilian he saw as best used in the context of rational debate, as in his essays.

In the wake of Spain's loss of Cuba in 1898 and the crisis that followed, he produced a ferocious condemnation of the colonial wars in his 'Oda a Espanya' ('Ode to Spain', written in Catalan):

> Listen, Spain, hear the voice of one of your sons
> Speaking to you in a voice that is not Castilian;
> I speak the language given to me by these harsh lands,
> A language few have used to speak to you. [. . .]

Why so much blood spilt needlessly?
Blood is life, life for today and for those to come.
Spilled blood is death. You thought too much about honour
And barely about life and you delivered your sons
To a tragic death.
You were satisfied with mortal honours;
Funerals were your celebrations.
Oh, sad Spain! I saw boats [. . .]
Sailing towards death; they travelled into the unknown,
Smiling, and you sang by the sea like a crazed old hag.
Where are your boats now? Where are your sons?

His spiritualism was more orthodox and more conservative than others in the movement. One of his most famous poems, 'Ode to Barcelona', celebrates the city's growth and development and the bourgeoisie that brought it about, *his* bourgeoisie. But the emphasis he places in the poem is on unity and a healing of social divisions, a theme to which he returned frequently. In 1909 he was writing his Ode to Barcelona when the events of July that year, the Semana Trágica or Tragic Week, interrupted him.

The Semana Trágica was one more expression of the simmering and unresolved discontent that pervaded Barcelona throughout the first decade of the twentieth century. The shock of 1898, and the sight of the returning defeated troops that had so moved Maragall, was not resolved then or later, but had two effects. On the one hand, the resentment and frustration of the poor were deepened, when they returned to conditions unchanged from before they had boarded ship for Africa and the Caribbean. And on the other, the defeat of 1898 struck fear into a middle class who anticipated explosions of social rage at any time. The political expression of the middle class's position was the support given to the conservative and conciliatory (with Madrid) Lliga Regionalista, led by Francesc Cambó, in 1901. In 1903, however, a general strike was called by the anarchist trade unions, anticipating that the protest would spread beyond Cataluña against the background of Spain's loss of its overseas empire. But the government played the separatist card, characterising the rising as nationalist rather than insurrectionary. The support from the rest of Spain did not come, and the strike movement was then isolated and brutally put down. Barcelona's bourgeoisie breathed easily again in its returning prosperity; still nothing was resolved.

The explosion of popular frustration in 1909, however, was not so easily contained. The reaction of the authorities to the anti-war demonstrations on the Ramblas in July (discussed in Chapter 6), and to the church burnings that followed, was brutal and repressive. The execution of the educationalist Francisco Ferrer, an important anarchist thinker who had in fact been absent from the city during those events, provoked widespread protests inside and outside Spain. The second part of Maragall's 'Ode to Barcelona' is an appeal to the authorities to save Ferrer's life as well as those of the other five anarchists who had been arrested. He sent the poem to the newspaper, *La Voz de Barcelona,* but the editor, the leader of the conservative Lliga Regionalista, Prat de la Riba, refused to publish it. In the end, Maragall accepted the decision; his protest was an appeal on ethical grounds, a call for an act of kindness which he felt, as a religious man, was the natural response of a Christian. It was not a gesture of rebellion or opposition. Although he later publicly distanced himself from *noucentrisme*, the movement that challenged Modernisme in the name of order and reason, it was for artistic and aesthetic reasons – a defence of poetry rather than of revolution. After 1909, Maragall withdrew into his family circle and died two years later.

A year later, in 1910, the man whose name has become synonymous with Barcelona, Antoni Gaudí, completed the building that was probably the high point of his work and the final pinnacle of Modernista architecture – the Casa Milà in the Paseo de Gracia, more generally known by the not entirely complimentary name La Pedrera, which means the stone quarry.

It is impossible to write about Barcelona without including Gaudí, whose work is probably the major attraction for at least half the city's visitors. Gaudí was an artist in every sense, an inspired architect, an admirer of the craftspeople of Cataluña, a visionary – but he was not greatly interested in literature and, strangely, has not figured as a character in fiction (an exception is a rather poor recent novel on the *Da Vinci Code* model). Perhaps he was simply too large and complex a figure to be contained within any one volume! Yet it would be absurd not to include him in this companion. He is mentioned, of course, by visitors to the city. George Orwell was very rude about the Sagrada Familia (of which more in a moment) and recommended during the Civil War that revolutionaries and anarchists should get rid of it. A great deal of damage was done to the buildings during the Civil War, but for anti-religious rather than aesthetic reasons. John Langdon-Davies, in *Behind the Spanish Barricades* (1937), described it in its 'full horror' as 'anarcho-syndicalism in architecture' (though the anarchists clearly did not agree).

Gaudí belonged to the Modernisme movement artistically, but he shared none of the progressive, Bohemian ideas of the original clients of the Quatre Gats. However, after the café was closed in 1903 it was reopened as the headquarters of the Sant Lluc Circle, of which Gaudí was a co-founder. In *Barcelona*, Robert Hughes describes the group as 'an aggressively conservative and religious association of artists, sculptors, architects and decorators'. Its guide and mentor was the bishop of Vic, Josep Torras i Bagas, probably the most influential right-wing religious thinker of his time. For Bagas, materialism and art were sworn enemies. Realism was the saboteur of art's divine and visionary purpose, which in his view was to celebrate and acknowledge the work of God, while Modernisme was 'neurotic and immoral'. In this, he and Gaudí, as well as Maragall, were in agreement.

Rafael Paget, who knew Gaudí, is quoted in Josep Pla's *Un senyor de Barcelona* (*A Man of Barcelona*, 1977):

His personality was driven by a morbid and incurable pride. In a country where most things have still to be achieved and what is done is always in danger of being torn down or remaining unfinished, our architect had an innate originality and worked as if architecture had appeared at the moment when he arrived on the face of the earth. [For him] the purpose was not to create an architecture that responded to human life but rather one that was an imitation of the cosmic life in which people lived a mystical-troglodytic experience [. . .] Gaudí is neither Roman nor Catholic in the sense in which those words are generally understood in our culture. He is a primitive Christian from the forest.

For Maragall, who saw art and religion as a celebration of what was positive and purposeful in human life, Gaudí's vision was driven by a notion of punishment and repentance that the poet found far too negative. That is certainly the spirit that pervades the Sagrada Familia. Yet his early work is in every sense a celebration of nature in its multiple forms (nature as the work of the divine), of the craftsmanship of his native Cataluña, and of its history.

Gaudí was born in the town of Reus, near Tarragona, in 1852, to a family of *caldereros*, metalworkers. His profound religious feelings were obvious at a very early age; his first architectural project was for a restoration of the emblematic Poblet monastery near his home. In 1878, Eusebio Guell – said at the time to be the tenth richest man in the world, with a dominant position in the Catalan industrial bourgeoisie – attended a trade fair in Paris and saw there a cabinet made by Gaudí for a glove manufacturer. Its combination of moulded and carved wood and stained glass fascinated him, and he returned to seek out the young architect, whose patron and financial support he then became. Most of what Gaudí created thereafter bore the name of Guell, or of the equally wealthy Milà or Batlló families.

The Guell Palace, off the Ramblas, and the Guell Park, over-looking the city, are riveting examples of Gaudí's artistry and of his revival of great local crafts like *trancadís* – the use of broken ceramics to interrupt, decorate and colour the basic building materials – had a long history. Gaudí's spiritual devotion to nature was the basis of an approach which found ways of reproducing the lines and shapes of nature in buildings and structures in urban settings. The Casa Milà, for example, seen from within or without or from the breath-taking roof garden (if that is the right word for it) is a sweeping moving sequence of curved and mobile lines. For all the primitivism they may have expressed, his structures were remarkable pieces of engineering as well as works of art. Technically speaking, the Casa Milà is unfinished. Gaudí wanted to hang a huge statue of the Virgin on the façade as a final touch. Milà, though a practising Catholic, thought it too provocative so soon after the events of the Tragic Week, and refused.

The Sagrada Familia became the obsession of the eccentric and ageing Gaudí. The irony, of course, is that the world has come to the building, bemused perhaps by its eccentricity and by its sheer artistic – but not worldly – ambition. As you climb the towers – use the stairs if you can, rather than the lift – you are taken through

7 *The façade of Antoni Gaudí's emblematic Casa Milà, in Barcelona's Paseo de Gracia*

gardens and forests, past curves and arabesques, into and out of space, across bridges hanging in mid-air, and at every turn there will be some reminder in stone of nature's ingenuity. As a project, though, it seems all but impossible, especially when there were no drawings – it was all in the head of Gaudí, who lived on a sparse vegetarian diet in a shed within the cathedral site. The Casa Milà is, in Michael Eaude's view, 'both the peak of modernism and its last great building. The Sagrada Familia, by contrast, surprising though it is, is pastiche, decadence and religious mania.'

Then and now, Gaudí's work provoked fierce debate. Evelyn Waugh, visiting in 1929, said that 'the glory and enchantment of Barcelona, which no other city in the world can offer, is the architecture of Gaudí', while Orwell and Langdon-Davies both scorned the building, and Orwell hoped someone would knock it down. But millions have come to see it, to climb the towers and gasp at its sheer ambition, even though ambition was the last thing that drove Gaudí. Those involved in its completion, a process that will probably take one more generation, are working from hints and clues – there are no plans and the model Gaudí made was smashed during the Civil War. His plan was in his head, and died with him under a tram. He had no followers – unsurprisingly, given the complexity and explosiveness of his vision. But he was nonetheless a member of a generation that included other major architects. Unexpectedly, perhaps, the most representative of Modernist architects, Le Corbusier, was an admirer of Gaudí:

What I saw in Barcelona – Gaudí – was the work of a man with extraordinary strength, faith and technical skill, manifested throughout a life spent on site, a man who had the stones carved under his supervision, according to drawings of great wisdom. Gaudí is the 'builder' of 1900, a craftsman, a builder in stone, iron and brick. He is now honoured in his own country. Gaudí was a great artist; only those who touch the most sensitive parts of the hearts of men last and will last. But at a halfway point they will be mistreated, misunderstood and accused of the sin of being a momentary fashion [. . .] but they will triumph [. . .] for architecture is a product, a manifestation, of character.

Modernisme produced at least two other architects whose achievements could be compared with those of Gaudí. The Block of Discord, on the Paseo de Gracia, includes a building by each of the three. Though the crowds mass around Gaudí's very beautiful Casa Batlló, both Lluis Domènech i Montaner and Puig i Cadafalch's buildings, each very different in style, are masterworks in the Catalan style. Indeed Modernisme, as Robert Hughes points out, had reached a point of exhaustion by 1910 or so, though Gaudí continued for another two decades in his own extraordinary individual project. In an important respect, as Hughes says, 'Gaudí was not a Moderniste architect at all. His religious obsessions, for instance, separate him from the generally secular character of modernisme. Gaudí did not believe in modernity. He wanted to find radically new ways of being radically old: a fiercer project altogether.'

Domènech's design for the Palau de la Música Catalá, in Carrer Sant Pere Mais Alt, is an emblematic building in the Catalan cultural renaissance (with a small 'r'). It is many ways a homage to Anselm Clavé, who rediscovered and celebrated Catalan popular music. Michael Eaude underlines the contrast between the Liceu, which was essentially built to cater for the musical tastes of the Catalan middle classes – Italian opera and then later, Wagner – and the Palau. Clavé, in contrast to Domènech, was committed to a more popular and more democratic Catalan culture, and the Orfeo Catalá, as the Palau is also known, has been and remains an arena for a wider and more accessible range of music. The building itself has all the features of Modernisme, inside and out. But within Modernisme itself music was a focus of passionate dispute. The musical radicals who brought Erik Satie and others to Sitges, however, were highly critical of what they felt was the paternalistic and sometimes sentimental view of the productions of the Orfeo. But they would no doubt have been pleased at the events of 1960, when a choir sang the banned Catalan hymn to the Catalan flag, 'La Senyera', with Franco in the audience. The organiser of the concert, Jordi Pujol, was arrested and jailed for the insult to the Franco regime, even though he had not been present. He later became president of Cataluña before his questionable financial dealings undermined his reputation as a Catalan radical.

Robert Hughes describes the Orfeo as 'Wagnerian' in its boldness and its scale and in its gathering together of all the arts in one overwhelming, crowded mythical space – as might be said of any of the Ring Cycle operas. Wagner's immense popularity among the wealthier idle classes at the turn of the century had much to do with the combination of epic features, an almost medieval mysticism and extravagant performance. A visit to the main concert hall to hear a concert is an overpowering experience. Hughes describes it as being 'saturated with sound', but it is the combination of light, sound, sculpture and atmosphere that leaves one breathless. The whole sense is of a floating world, reinforced by the winged horses arrested in flight on either side of the stage; they form part of a proscenium arch dedicated to an 'Allegory of Catalan Music' which embraces Beethoven and Clavé as well as flowers and trees of the Catalan countryside. It is especially surprising because the building, squeezed into a small site on Sant Pere Mais Alt, just off the Via Layetana, barely allows the visitor to see the full extent of its façade – the impact is reserved to those who enter.

Domènech was also the designer and architect of the Hospital de Sant Pau, not far from the Sagrada Familia but as distant from it as is imaginable in terms of its purpose and content. The hospital is much closer to the philosophy that had moved Cerdà in his original designs for the Eixample, in the sense that environment and surroundings have a direct effect on human health. This idea that 'bienestar es terapia' ('well-being is therapy') was built into the Sant Pau, also completed in 1910. At the time Barcelona had no general hospital. Domènech, as many have since acknowledged, avoided the geometric lines of the Eixample, which could be oppressive, preferring diagonals and wards separated by green spaces. And, to dissociate the hospital from the idea of death, the entrance is bathed in light reflected through the coloured glass of the dome. By the twenty-first century, the hospital was conserved as an architectural space, though the attached hospital buildings were more conventional and less spacious.

Domènech was the very opposite of the isolated hermit of the Sagrada Familia. Like Gaudí, he worked with teams of artists and craftsmen, but where Gaudí was intractable and authoritarian, Domènech was a public figure comfortable in the political and social life of the city. He was engaged in a multitude of activities, and his social awareness is manifest in the design of the Sant Pau hospital. All his work is within Cataluña: though he travelled in Europe, he did not build elsewhere. He was in any event a dedicated Catalanist, but of a conservative nature. He is one more example of the curious Catalan combination of political conservatism combined with an admiration for the popular and an adventurous artistic spirit.

Perhaps for the same reason, Barcelona was a magnet for a wider avant-garde, often forgotten beside the overpowering public presence of Modernisme. The Sitges circle had invited Débussy and Satie to their gatherings, and Arnold Schönberg and Igor Stravinsky – as well as the Ballets Russes company which spent time in the city in the years before World War I. The Delmau Gallery, then in Carrer Puertaferrisa off the Ramblas, held a Cubist exhibition. Joan Miró and Dalí were clearly aware of, and touched by, avant-garde artistic currents. After 1914, many writers, painters and musicians sought temporary refuge in the city too: Breton, Picabia and Apollinaire among them.

As Modernisme faded, in the context of an increasingly conservative politics exemplified by the Lliga led by Prat de la Riba and later Cambó, *noucentrisme* took its place. Literature and the visual arts returned to a kind of pastoral and confessional style, while the movement's architectural expressions were classical, as in the Estación de Francia or the new Via Layetana, which swept down from the Plaza Urquinaona to the port, demolishing hundreds of buildings in the La Ribera district that stood in its way.

The Modernist architects Le Corbusier and Ludwig Mies van der Rohe visited Barcelona at the end of the 1920s. Mies van der Rohe's pavilion at the 1929 Exposition expressed a very different, international Modernism. Demolished after 1929, it has been rebuilt on the site above the Plaza d'Espanya. Le Corbusier advised the new Republican government in 1931 on its housing plan, but there was no time to develop his ideas.

From 1939 onwards, fascism would dominate the city's culture, and return it to the curious combination of a profound conservatism on the one hand and a Modernist brutalism on the other. In some senses the eclectic Plaza Catalunya is a manifestation of that uncomfortable combination, with the 'oceanliner' of the Corte Inglés department store as the remaining representative of Mayor Josep Porcioles's vision of a modern city under Franco.

 5

THE RAVAL:
SEX AND REVOLUTION

The Raval, known as the Chinese Quarter or, under Franco, District Five, begins from the Ramblas and stretches to the Paralelo on its other edge. It was always a place of outsiders. Incorporated into the old city with the third extension of the wall in 1355, it remained an area of Church lands and market gardens. The immigrants and marginals who clustered around the wall – the Gypsies, fortune-tellers, butchers, ropemakers, prostitutes and criminals – were shut out of the city at night. But in the eighteenth century the city's growth drew new populations, particularly as textile manufacture increased in importance and the port became a significant trading centre.

The Conde de Asalto's expansion of the city into the Raval in the late eighteenth century, paving the Ramblas and building new streets through the warren of alleys that had grown up there over time, was an immediate response to the overcrowding of the old town. The new streets emerged quickly, at least until 1807, when the Napoleonic invasion put the process on hold until 1817. But the proliferation of new industrial plants and the rapid growth of the immigrant population transformed it very quickly into an area whose population density was the highest in Europe. A report by Dr Joaquín Font Mosella described the area in 1852:

Barcelona was reduced to the tight circle of the walls, while the majority of the market gardens that in other times contributed to purifying the air, thanks to the oxygen that the plants emitted, were now transformed into magnificent factories or tiny habitations. The modest houses, once only one or two floors high, now rose to a third or a fourth; the newer flats once occupied by a single family were converted into several small rooms and their rents considerably increased, following the astonishing increase in the value of the land. The wretched workers are forced to live crowded together in tiny and unventilated rooms, suffering the consequences of incomplete renovations and contaminated air [. . .] Last month the political newspapers carried reports of a house in the San Antonio district which despite its restricted size accommodated on its five floors one hundred and fifteen people, the majority of them factory workers.

It was assumed that the modernisation of the area on both sides of the Ramblas early in the nineteenth century would attract the middle classes to Carrer Ferran and the elegant Plaza Reial, but the building of the Eixample and the development of the Paseo de Gracia proved altogether more tempting. In any event, the densely overcrowded housing of the Raval, interspersed with factories where many of the inhabitants worked, plus the scant attention paid to public health or the education of the population, ensured that the area would continue to be home to the poor and marginalised. By the second half of the nineteenth century the textile plants were larger and more highly mechanised and were already moving out of the Raval to suburban areas such as Sants and Sant Andreu. Within the Raval it was small workshops – printing shops, joineries, distilleries – that remained, plus the growing population of bars, café-concerts, theatres, dance halls and brothels – in one guise or another – centred on streets like Trentaclaus (later Arc de Teatre) and Hospital. The reality was that prostitution was a major industry in the district, just as it had been before the expansion. The population of the Raval at the turn of the century, as described by Pierre Villar in *Historia y leyenda del Barrio Chino* (*History and*

8 A street in the Raval district, known as the Barrio Chino or Chinese Quarter

Legends of the Chinese Quarter, 1996), read like a portrait of the Court of Miracles:

> The Raval, and above all the area around Drassanes, harboured a separate world, a world with its own codes and its own morality, with its own heterogenous criminal class, 'pintxos' or pimps from the gambling dens, metal thieves, cigarette smugglers, whores, cat burglars, pickpockets, 'errand boys' (probably runners for the drug traffickers), beggars. In that world it was the law of the survival of the fittest, the most macho, that prevailed. And even for the police it was dangerous territory.

It may have been risky for the middle class or the police to go into the area at that stage, but the Raval's population encountered them regularly on the Ramblas, a kind of common space where the rich and the poor would, and still do, mingle. The Ramblas were a space for strolling and enjoying the shopping opportunities that the later nineteenth century brought. It was also the frequent site of demonstrations, fights between rival gangs or between prostitutes, their clients and their pimps. The middle classes at the turn of the century preferred to promenade along the Paseo de Gracia.

The Growth of Anarchism

The city was continuing its metamorphosis, but the atmosphere as the new century began was increasingly tense, especially since the anarchist bombings of the previous decade. The syndicalist current in anarchism was growing in influence among workers, especially in the Raval, as the general strike in 1902 demonstrated. But it was a critical event in 1909 that exposed the depth of the social divide.

The mayor of Barcelona, Angel Ossorio y Gallardo, in a personal memoir of the events, *Barcelona julio de 1909* (*Barelona, July 1909*) published the following year, gave a revealing assessment of the events:

> I don't know how revolutions are made elsewhere. I imagine a group of fearsome men meet in some mysterious bar; that they silently recruit; that the leaders communicate among themselves using a secret language, disguising their ideas and their bodies too. In those circumstances we can discuss what the authorities could have done to stop them.
>
> But in Barcelona? Anyone who says that the authorities could or should have known that a revolution was coming doesn't know what they are talking about [. . .] In Barcelona, the revolution is not prepared, quite simply because it is always ready and waiting. It appears every day in the street; if the time isn't right it steps back, if it is, it happens.

Ossorio was right, and the proof came, a year later, in June 1910 when the new anarchist workers' federation, the Confederación Nacional del Trabajo (CNT), was founded in the city with 75,000 members.

The Tragic Week, La Semana Trágica, began on 26 July 1909 with a demonstration against the war in Morocco. The Madrid government was persuaded by the powerful Count of Romanones, owner of an iron mine in independent Morocco, to send detachments of soldiers from the Spanish enclave of Melilla to defend the mine from the local Rif tribes. Thus Spain launched yet another Moroccan campaign, sending 40,000 troops effectively to invade Morocco. The sight of young men marching down the Ramblas to the port was a reminder of the events of 1898. And when Claudio López, the son of the hugely wealthy Marquis of Comillas, a banker with his own interests in the mine, arrived at the port with the wealthy ladies of the Eixample to distribute rosaries and scapularies among the recruits, it was too much for the families of the Raval, Poble Nou and the Barceloneta from which they came. These were the same families who had seen their husbands and sons sent to Cuba and return – if they returned at all – ravaged by disease, mutilated and demoralised.

Between 14 and 18 July 1909, women and children gathered daily on the Ramblas and at the port, trying to pull back their sons, husbands and fathers. They hurled insults at the patriotic marches played at the waterside by military bands, and many of those who had fought in the previous decade threw their medals into the sea. The Civil Guard attacked the demonstrations. On the 19th the anarchist regional federation organised its own march down the Ramblas and issued a call for a general strike. On 26 July the strike took place and was almost completely successful. Only the trams continued to run, driven largely by immigrants. The government then declared a state of emergency and troops appeared on the streets. The strike continued, but the organising committee lost control of events as the repression intensified. Thirty churches were burned before the Semana ended. On 17 August, the first executions took place.

Eight religious buildings were burned, between 75 and 100 people killed, and hundreds jailed. Francisco Ferrer, an anarchist educator with an international reputation, was arrested and later executed at Montjuich, though he had not even been present in Barcelona during the events. A wave of repression followed, directed particularly again the working-class organisations, although they had effectively lost control of events after the second day. The execution of Ferrer brought widespread protest, even from those who would not necessarily have sympathised with the strike, such as the mystical poet Joan Maragall:

Does your heart not speak to you when they are shooting people on Montjuich solely because they manifested more clearly the disease that we all suffer from? Doesn't your heart tell you that you should ask forgiveness, on your knees if possible, and first among you the most offended, for those of our brothers without love who wanted to reduce to earth this city that we in our egoism had abandoned? They will have to pay the price because they acted according to a code, whereas our inaction is so worthless that it belongs to no one? Go and ask forgiveness of human justice on their behalf, which will be the same as asking it for yourselves, because before God you are even more guilty than they.

The combination of anti-militarism and anti-clericalism among workers, together with their harsh treatment at the hands of the Barcelona employers, proved to be an explosive mix. However, Barcelona remained the centre of a growing and profitable textile industry, together with ironworks and construction, attracting a flow of immigrants from Murcia, Valencia and Aragon.

Eduardo Mendoza's Onofre Bouvila, the central character of Mendoza's *City of Marvels*, seems characteristically unconcerned when the Marquis of Ut rushes into his house in a panic:

'We're done for,' he exclaimed, his hair dishevelled, his tie undone. 'The provincial governor refuses to declare a state of emergency, the mob is ruling the streets, the churches are all ablaze, and Madrid as usual, has left us high and dry.'

Onofre extended to him an embossed leather box full of Havanas. 'Nothing will come of it. At worst your palace might be burned down. Is your family out of the country?'

'They're spending the summer on the coast at Sitges,' said the marquis.

'And your palace, is it insured?'

'Of course.'

'Well, there you are. Take my advice, go and spend a few days with your wife and children.'

Onofre is an archetypal venture capitalist, alive to every new opportunity, however murky, and always prepared to use whatever means necessary to ensure his position and feather his already very luxurious nest. The world was changing and the futuristic dreams of the visionaries of the *fin de siècle* seemed now much closer: flight, electricity, urban transport. But Onofre sees the most profitable opportunity in the preparations for war that his spies tell him are afoot in Germany, where the Krupp factories are forging the weapons of the future. In August 1913, just one year before the outbreak of World War I, Onofre stands at the docks watching the unloading of mysterious crates that contained 'the prototypes of the rifles, grenades, mortars and flamethrowers' that he would manufacture in this new economic boom promised by war.

But in 1913, when Onofre was receiving his secret cargo, war was still a year away. The industrial bourgeoisie seemed at that stage to be most committed to the growth of the city itself, as it expanded further into the surrounding areas such as Gracia, Horta and Sants. The Via Layetana, built in 1907, was more Wall Street than Champs Elysées, reflecting a dominant culture of order and a commitment to business and finance. The wealthier families looked further and higher, towards the Collserolla where the electric tram groaned its way up the Avinguda Tibidabo (and still does), past the grand houses (*torres*) of the new aristocracy, to the foot of the funicular railway that takes the visitor to the Church of the Sagrado Corazón

(Sacred Heart) at the top of the hill. The church was built in 1902 in imitation of its namesake in Paris, the Sacré Coeur of Montmartre, itself raised in gratitude for the containment of popular rebellion after the defeat of the Paris Commune in 1871.

Bohemia Comes to the Raval

Spain was not involved in World War I, but it profited from what was happening in the rest of Europe. The war transformed the Raval in several ways. The industrial expansion attracted waves of new immigrants who came to live in the Raval, on Montjuich or the other poor areas of the city. The city drew other migrants too – the artists and writers who fled to Spain to avoid the war. It was they who would be responsible for the creation of the myth of the Raval as a place of decadence, transgression, rampant sexuality, the perverse and the forbidden, which attracted other Bohemian travellers in the following decade. At the same time the city became a magnet for other, less salubrious visitors, the spies and counter-spies of either side, the legendary Mata Hari, confidence tricksters and speculators as well as black marketeers. The sex business boomed, and Barcelona enjoyed a monopoly in the production of pornography. The writer Manuel Vázquez Montalbán, who was brought up in the Raval, described this process in *Barcelonas* (1992) as 'the internationalization of the district', both in the sense that many foreigners came to visit or live there, and that the Raval began to enjoy a reputation for the forbidden, the perverse and the promiscuous that spread well beyond its frontiers, as a kind of successor to Paris's Montmartre.

> Barcelona became a magnet for people from every latitude, voluntary and forced emigrants, adventurers and smugglers, traffickers and spies. Every kind of business could prosper there, mercenary love was on offer in industrial quantities, pimping needed no planning and drugs and alcohol found an open space for expansion. Contraband

whisky appeared, driving away the more innocent local brews. Everything from textiles to rabbit skins were sent to France and millions came back, creating work for three shifts in the factories, for the cattle rustlers in the Pyrenees, for the croupiers in the casinos, the comedians in the theatres, the tango dancers in the clubs and for available women everywhere [. . .] The money made in business flowed back towards a manic epicureanism, dances, gambling and naked women.

This was war as economic boom, as Marcelino Moreta describes it in his 1971 *Historias de Barcelona* (*Barcelona Stories*). The attention this brought was not always desirable. The proliferation of cafés, bars, brothels and burlesque theatre reflected the growing numbers of working-class women drawn into prostitution in its many forms by poverty and the loss of their menfolk in foreign wars. The red-light zone was a no man's land for the moralists and the forces of order, but it was a brutal place to which the new clientele had brought jazz, cinema and electric light. They also brought hard drugs, especially cocaine, child prostitution and the proliferating exploitation of women along with modish new drinks like whisky and cherry flips. Almost anything contraband could be bought or sold on the streets of the Chinese Quarter, the Barrio Chino.

On the Paralelo some of the key names of that era are still there in lights. El Molino (The Mill) was called Le Moulin until Franco declared all foreign words anathema. It was the iconic vaudeville theatre through those years, though it opened and closed several times. Around the corner, the infamous Bagdad offered live sex shows as well as striptease and song – and still does. One by-product of these wild years was the growing enthusiasm for the flamenco music and dance of southern Spain, which continues to be seen around the city.

Joan Castells (in Paco Villar's book on the Barrio Chino) described the Paralelo:

From the point of view of entertainment, Paralelo offered every kind; café-concerts, restaurants, bars. It became a popular centre where you could take the pulse of the city's social and political life. The orchestra at the grand Café Espanyol, frequented essentially by the working class, included classical music in its weekly repertoire. But the Paralelo was also where the first barricades would go up whenever there was conflict.

For this was the special and paradoxical nature of the Raval. It was a pleasure zone for some, but it was also the area where anarchism took root and gave birth to its most combative expressions. The CNT, for example, by 1918 could claim 250,000 members in Cataluña. The factories of Barcelona were rarely still during those years. The increasing strength and militancy of the trade unions, dominated by the CNT, were certainly an unintended consequence of that growth, but an inevitable one, given that the priority was to keep production going at all costs.

The protests called early in 1917 by the CNT, among others, mobilised a working class who had derived few benefits from the financial and commercial boom that enriched Onofre Bouvila and his ilk. The 1917 action began as a 'subsistence strike', in protest at the rising cost of food. It was at its most determined in Barcelona. The Franco-Russian writer Victor Serge had arrived in Barcelona directly from imprisonment in France, where he had been sentenced for involvement in an anarchist bank robbery (in which he had in fact not participated). His novel *Birth of Our Power* (1931) is set in the early months of 1917 in the febrile atmosphere of an industrial city. Serge found work in a printshop, where he met with political exiles like himself and with the anarchist union leaders. His central character, Darío, is clearly based on the legendary CNT leader Salvador Segui, known as the 'noi de la sucre' ('the sugar boy') because of his habit of eating the sugar cubes that came with his coffee. Segui was later assassinated, in 1923, but Serge repeatedly suggests that he was permanently in danger and aware of his exposure; and that that served only to underline his courage and selflessness. In fact, Segui himself wrote a novel, *Escuela de rebeldía* (*School for Rebels*, 1923), which was clearly autobiographical; its central character is a dedicated revolutionary and trade union organiser who is killed. It was published two weeks after Segui was murdered on Carrer de la Cadena in the Raval, on the very spot where his protagonist had died.

Serge's novel is part of a series born out of his own experience as a witness to historic events in which he was at once a participant and a sharp critical observer. In *Birth of Our Power* the protagonists are collective, groups of people sharing experiences and purposes, workers living at moments of dramatic change, even if, as in 1917, their impact could only be imagined – or sensed.

Serge's descriptions of the city are powerful and evocative. More than mere background, the city is an active, living organism in which Serge and his friends are sometimes adrift and sometimes bound together by past experiences and by a sense of transience, of change:

> I had learned in the city that it was not enough to fill your life with the certainty of not being killed by the end of the day [. . .] It often happened, during my strolls on the Montjuich rock, that I had the sensation of being at one with the earth's extremities, which resulted in a strange despondency. There, facing the horizon or during night walks through the happy city, this feeling – usually indistinct within me – attained a sombre clarity. The peace we were enjoying was unique, and that city, despite the struggles, the pain, the filth hidden away in her hunger-ridden slums [. . .] was more than happy just to be alive. We were, nonetheless, only a hundred miles from the Pyrenees; on the other side was the other universe, ruled over by the cannons.

The movement was preparing for a battle of a different order, a struggle in the streets. Serge recognised the deep commitment of those who were preparing to strike, 'their burning dreams ready to become acts because men of energy live by them'. With characteristic honesty, he also sees the fragility that is a consequence of their lack of organisation. There were still only a few thousand union members among the city's 150,000 workers.

In the novel the strike itself occupies just one chapter, ominously titled 'Ebb Tide', and it is crushed by the violent attacks of the Civil Guard. Yet the leaders, like Darío, refuse to accept that it is a defeat. For Serge, the strike had all the elements of tragedy, but a tragedy that was both heroic and pregnant with future possibilities despite everything. He foresees a 'tomorrow full of greatness' when 'this city will be taken, if not by our hands, at least by others like ours, but stronger'. Among the group of exiles, the news of the revolution in Russia in 1917 renews their hope, even in the wake of defeat. Serge leaves Spain to return to the Russia of his birth, and another city, Petrograd: 'from a country where the flame is smouldering under the ashes to a country in flames'. His journey would be fraught with difficulties and it was a year before he reached Petrograd.

In Paris Serge had been in contact with the Russian avant-garde artists in exile from Czarism. With the revolution, like Serge, many of them would return – though the flowering of Modernism in Russia would last just over a decade before it was suppressed. Serge's narrative style echoes that movement; expressionistic rather than realist, it is a prose of light and shadow, dramatic portraits and lyrical description, at the heart of which is a profound humanism and the resilience of hope. *Birth of Our Power* was published in 1931, when the Stalinism of which Serge was a relentless critic had appropriated the Russian Revolution (he would later describe his terrible experience of exile to Siberia in *Midnight in the Century*, 1939).

In Barcelona, as in most European industrial cities with large bodies of workers, the Russian Revolution had an enormous impact. As Ono-fre Bouvila notes in Mendoza's *City of Marvels,* the approaching era of revolution frightened the powerful members of Barcelona's ruling elite. In the novel they meet in secret and wearing masks – but Onofre is sceptical and suspicious of their plans, though they remain unclear, until he looks beneath the table and notes that the most authoritative speaker is wearing military boots. It is a sign of things to come.

Eduardo Mendoza's *La verdad sobre el caso Savolta* (*The Truth About the Savolta Case*, 1975) is a novel set in the Barcelona of 1917 and gives a powerful sense of the atmosphere of conflict in the city, but from the opposite side from Serge. The economy is booming – the Savolta arms factory is one of its beneficiaries. The trade unions are growing too, and the Savolta plant is not exempt from their impact. The actions of 1917 were, as it emerged, a prelude to the major confrontation two years later. The manager of the Savolta factory, a slightly mysterious Frenchman called Lepprince, hires some small-time thugs to threaten and assault the strike leaders. *The Truth About the Savolta Case* flows from this initial act and its multiple consequences.

Like most of Mendoza's writings, the novel has a series of different narrative voices. It is what gives his fictions set in the real history of Barcelona their strength; events are interpreted in many different ways and from the place where each belongs in the complex social arrangements of the growing city. Lepprince functions among the factory owners, for whom the growth of anarchism among the workers is a threat to their luxurious lives – depicted with a wealth of detail by Mendoza. It is always the detail that gives his writing its fullness. The radical journalist Pajarito de Soto is given to regular denunciations of the rich in his articles and investigations for his newspaper the *Voice of Justice*; yet it is Lepprince who offers him the chance to investigate the attacks on workers that he himself has organised.

As the narrative moves between the Eixample (where the rich live) to the Chinese Quarter, the background gallery of characters fills out the historical record and explains the anger that prevails in the conflict between the two Barcelonas. The police inspector, Vasquez, provides his own deposition, while retrospective detail – an interrogation by an American judge – is added by the central witness to all these events, Javier Miranda. He is a clerk to Lepprince's lawyer, who is later adopted by the Frenchman to be his unwitting instrument. Javier is the fall guy in a complex intrigue which, until the end of the war and the collapse of the factory, the Frenchman manipulates like a puppet master. Javier is an innocent surrounded by corrupt and hypocritical people – and with a deep romantic streak that makes him especially vulnerable to the beautiful acrobat to whom he is attached in a marriage of convenience (convenient for Lepprince, that is). The chase in the novel's final part is classic melodrama – even down to the horse-drawn carriage taking his lover, Maria, away with another man, and the lorry carrying eight women and a message of free love that gets him home to Barcelona in the end. These touches of derring-do and romantic adventure are typical of Mendoza's writing, always graced with an element of self-parody and an ironic but affectionate portrait of working-class life.

The Truth About the Savolta Case is in some sense a prelude to the larger novel, *City of Marvels*, which shares some of its characters, and both Savolta and Bouvila are arms manufacturers. Together they provide a panorama of a city in transition during which its hidden conflicts rise to the surface.

The novel was published in April 1975, just before the death of Franco. As Mendoza says in his introduction to the novel:

> It was a time of feverish anticipation; a system that had seemed immovable was breaking up before our eyes and change, however uncertain, was imminent [. . .] The population lived in a state of permanent alert, not just because of political events, but in response to anything that was happening. Public opinion was highly sensitive [. . .] and in contrast to previous decades, people avidly read the newspapers and magazines and reflected on them.

There were obvious parallels between the two moments in Barcelona's history, moments of imminent and unpredictable change.

Class Warriors

The first postwar test of strength between capital and labour came at the Three Chimneys plant (the chimneys are still there to be seen on Avenida Paralelo) of the Barcelona Traction and Light Company, known as La Canadiense after its Canadian owner,

Frank Pearson. When a number of its workers were dismissed for union activity early in 1919, the CNT called a strike in the gas and electricity industry for 5 February. Troops were called in to maintain production and the strike became general. It ended with an agreement after 44 days, but the city authorities did not honour the agreement, and a new strike was called for 24 March. This time it failed. Bizarrely, in April the government decreed the eight-hour working day, to begin on 1 October. When the time came for its implementation, however, the factory owners closed their plants for 12 days. The employers were flexing their muscles.

In the aftermath of the 1919 strike, the Raval was in every sense a very dangerous place. During the strike, the employers had gathered an armed civilian force to attack the strikers, known as the Sindicatos Libres (Free Unions). The infamous civil governor of Barcelona, Martínez Anido, launched an open war on anarchism, unleashing armed gangs in working-class areas. Their most famous victim, Salvador Segui (whom we have already met) was killed in 1923. A commemorative plaque in Montjuich cemetery records his life and death, but many more trade unionists and activists were murdered between 1920 and 1923. The assaults were met by an armed response from the anarchist ranks too. The tension in the streets took a heavy toll: 230 were killed in what was known as the '*pistoleros* war'. By April 1923, the bulk of the Catalan middle class willingly supported a military coup led by Miguel Primo de Rivera; in September of that year he was appointed by the king, Alfonso XIII, to lead the government in Madrid.

Those years were also boom times for the sex trade. Drugs were now freely available in the bars and brothels, and the French connection brought with it some more elegant houses; Madame Petit's was the most famous of them. The two worlds, anarchist organisation and commerce in sex, coexisted in the closed world of what one journalist, Francisco Madrid, baptised the Barrio Chino, the Chinese Quarter, after a visit to San Francisco's Chinatown – despite the fact that there were no Chinese families living there.

By the end of the 1920s, over 30 per cent of the population of the Raval were non-Catalans. Their presence, together with the Raval's not necessarily unjustified reputation as a centre of criminality, drug-taking and sexual perversion, a 'wild city', provoked fear and moral panic among some sectors of the bourgeoisie. For others – or perhaps the same people – it also exerted the fascination of the forbidden, the dark and the mysterious. It was what attracted Jean Genet – whose *A Thief's Journal* (1949) is mainly set in the Raval – and other members of the French avant-garde. It also drew in the wealthy members of the middle classes, whose journeys into the lower depths are so devastatingly represented in Josep Maria de Sagarra's emblematic novel of 1932, *Vida privada* (*Private Life*):

> Despite the interclass atmosphere that a few bourgeois and middle-class Bohemians in the pleasure spaces of the Paralelo created, there remained an abyss between those who sought out the primitive pleasures that the city centre offered and the industrial bourgeoisie that held publicly to elitist principles of deferred gratification, sobriety and respectability. The 'good citizens' frequently inveighed against the area bounded by the Paralelo and the Raval, describing it as a den of vice and corruption inhabited by sexual deviants, drug barons and the 'dangerous classes' who lived outside the law and who, in their view, should be kept under constant surveillance.

Barcelona had always received visitors from Europe and elsewhere. Writers such as Georges Bataille and Jean Genet had come to the city, and specifically to the Chinese Quarter, in search of sexual adventures and the dark underworld of the Raval. Genet's *A Thief's Journal* records his life as a thief and prostitute, his travels in the criminal underbelly of the city. The book is an exploration of the deviant and the perverse, a diary of passage through Europe: 'Abandoned by my family I already felt it was necessary to aggravate this condition by a preference for boys and this preference by theft, and theft by crime [. . .] I thus resolutely rejected a world that had rejected me.'

His life is a reversal of bourgeois morality, a reversal of the conventions and rules of a society that has rejected him. It is more than rebellion – he is wholly individualistic and pursues no ideals beyond the immediate pleasure he finds in submission, violence, the forbidden. His work would become especially popular in the 1960s. Jean Paul Sartre's monumental 1952 study of his work, *Saint Genet*, presented him as the embodiment of the amoral anti-hero. The Raval seemed to provide the environment where it was possible to live and survive in those terms.

The material for *A Thief's Journal* – part novel, part autobiography – was provided by Genet's life as a thief and a homosexual prostitute, which he began to narrate in his first autobiographical volume *Our Lady of the Flowers* (written in 1943, while in prison, but only published in 1951). In 1932, Genet found himself in Barcelona, and living in the Barrio Chino.

> Spain at this time was covered with vermin, its beggars [. . .] In Barcelona we hung around the Calle Mediodia and the Calle Carmen. We sometimes slept six in a bed without sheets, and at dawn we would go begging in the markets. We would leave the Barrio Chino in a group and scatter over the Paralelo, carrying shopping baskets, for the housewives would give us a leek or a turnip rather than a coin. At noon we would return and with the gleanings we would make our soup. It is the life of the vermin I am about to describe.

The aspect of the Barrio Chino which he describes became a standard view among some avant-garde circles. For Genet and Bataille the fascination of the Raval was its marginality, its moral emptiness, its fascinating horror, its human detritus. Both were journeying into a world of transgression, with Bataille especially fascinated by all that was perverse and humiliating. The Raval did contain all of these transgressions and perversions, as well as gay bars and ostentatious transvestites – but it was also more than this. The Chinese Quarter of Genet and Bataille, as Vázquez Montalbán pointedly suggests in his *Barcelonas*, was the creation of a European (and probably mainly Parisian) imagination:

> The Barrio Chino was, at the time, a kind of haunt thronged less with Spaniards than with foreigners, all of them down-and-out bums. We were sometimes dressed in almond-green or jonquil-yellow silk shirts and worn-out rope-soled sandals, and our hair was so plastered down that it looked as if it would crack [. . .] We did not form loosely organised bands, but amidst that vast, filthy disorder, in a neighbourhood stinking of oil, piss and shit, a few waifs and strays relied on others more clever than themselves. The squalor sparkled with the youth of many of our number and with the more mysterious brilliance of a few who really scintillated, youngsters whose bodies, gazes and gestures were charged with a magnetism which made of us their object.

The artists, writers and sexual tourists were drawn by a *nostalgie de la boue* which only made the place more seductive with each denunciation.

Chris Ealham's study of the anarchist movement in the city, *Anarchism and the City: Revolution and Counter-Revolution in Barcelona 1898–1937* (2010), however, shows a very different face of the Raval, as the heart of perhaps the most important and most successful anarchist project in Europe. The Raval was a place of poverty and human degradation but it was also the scene of determined and selfless efforts to raise the hopes and aspirations of ordinary people, a centre of political organisation as well as resistance.

The Raval had its own poet in Joan Salvat-Papasseit, who reflected both the political and the artistic radicalism that still flowered in the city. Born in 1894, he was orphaned at an early age and received a Catholic and military education at the Naval School. But as a young worker he was drawn to the active anarchist cultural circles in the Raval and attended the Ateneo Enciclopédico Popular in Carrer del Carme in the heart of the district. There he read the favoured writers of the age – Maxim Gorky, Henrik Ibsen, Georges Sorel, as well as the European Modernists like Marinetti and Apollinaire. From 1914 onwards he wrote regularly for the anarchist press, where he also began to publish his own poetry under the (significant) pseudonym 'Gorkiano'. The Uruguayan Modernist artist Torres-García was a friend who illustrated some of his poems, especially those after the style of Apollinaire. During those years, Salvat-Papasseit worked as a night watchman in the port, where his statue now stands on the Moll de la Fusta. He later found work in a bookshop and devoted himself to writing poetry, editing cultural journals and, from 1917, the newspaper *Un enemic del poble* (*An Enemy of the People*). He died of tuberculosis in 1924 at the age of 30. Later generations would discover that his poetry reflected a futuristic vocation:

> I invite you poets to be the future, that is, to be immortal, to sing about today, not to measure your verses nor to count them on your fingers, nor to demand money for them. We always live for what is to come, tomorrow is always more beautiful than yesterday and if you want to make rhymes, do it, but always be Poets, Poets with a capital P, arrogant, brave, heroic and above all true to yourselves.

Salvat-Papasseit's first book of poetry was called *Humo de fábrica* (*Factory Smoke*, 1918); seven more volumes appeared before his early death. A utopian and an anarchist, little of Salvat-Papasseit's poetry has been translated, but it resonates with his world and its inhabitants. His most famous poem, 'Nocturne for Accordion' (1926), dates from his time as a watchman on the docks; its opening lines are inscribed on the pedestal of his statue which overlooks the port:

> I've guarded wood at the docks;
> You don't know what it's like

To guard wood at the docks.
But I've seen the rain
Bucketing down
Drenching the boats [. . .]
You haven't heard
The prayer of the harbour lights
So many colours
Like the sea beneath the sun
That has no need of sails.

He was rediscovered in the 1960s by the iconic Catalan singer-songwriters Joan Manuel Serrat and Luis Llach, who set his poems to music, among them 'Visca l'amor' ('Long Live Love') and 'Res no es mesqui' ('Nothing is Paltry').

Salvat-Papasseit may appear as a rather isolated figure among the literary avant-garde. Yet his many books of poetry and his contributions, both political and literary, to a number of newspapers and journals set him in a different light. His audience were not the elite cultural circles of the city, but the different and equally vibrant cultural universe of the Raval. To the wider society of the city, anarchism appeared only as the force behind labour protests, trade union organisation and probably as fire-raisers.

In fact, the anarchist organisations were engaged in a whole range of educational and cultural activities in the working-class neighbourhoods. The impoverished population of the city, its immigrant workers in particular, lived in terrible conditions in the Raval, the Barri Gòtic and Barceloneta. They had little access to culture, which was limited to the city's middle classes, and education was exclusively under the control of the Church. School places were few and far between, and what schools there were were bitterly hostile to anarchist ideas. Francisco Ferrer's rationalist Modern School movement arose in opposition to the religious domination of education – and he was executed for those ideas rather than the false accusation of involvement in the uprising of 1909. The anarchist movement set out to provide both secular education and non-religious moral leadership, especially in relation to the condition of women. For example, the local community centres worked hard to provide alternatives for the women forced by poverty into prostitution. Chris Ealham's excellent book details the range of activities they encouraged – the literacy classes, theatrical and musical performances as well as discussions and debates. They also encouraged reading through the anarchist press or by printing cheap editions of classics. Zola was particularly popular, as was Gorky; both, after all, provided sympathetic portraits of working-class life.

The magazine *La novela ideal* (*The Ideal Novel*) began publishing in 1925 and continued on a regular basis (monthly at first, later weekly) until 1938. One of the series editors was the leading anarchist Federica Montseny, who would enter the Catalan government under Lluis Companys as a minister in 1936. *La novela ideal* published short novels, not political tracts. They were essentially uplifting stories about ordinary people, the very people who bought and read them. The paper said: 'We want to publish optimistic novels that fill the soul with hope; clean, serene, strong, they might provoke a curse, or a tear or two.' The implicit message was that these were alternatives to the romantic or the pornographic novels that circulated among the middle classes.

Published in 1932 but translated into English only in 2015, Josep Maria de Sagarra's gloriously satirical and iconoclastic novel *Private Life* is an acerbic and unforgiving portrait of Barcelona under the military dictatorship of Primo de Rivera (1923–30) and the first period of the Third Republic. Sagarra, who was born in 1894, was a prolific writer – a critic, journalist, playwright, novelist and poet. Like many young men from wealthy families, he studied law before abandoning it for literature. He spent the Civil War years outside Spain, but returned in 1940 to resume his writing career, and was eventually reconciled with and worked for the Franco regime.

Private Life is a journey through a city in a moment of its decadence. What remained of Cataluña's rural nobility had by the 1920s largely abandoned their ancestral lands and grand houses for Barcelona. Some had become members of a prosperous industrial middle class, investing what they had in the newer plants and factories in the city. Others immersed themselves in the shallow and trivial round of social engagements and mutual admiration that Sagarra paints with brutal precision. But in the relentless, breathless traffic of the social round, what Sagarra exposes is the shallowness of it all, and how little is revealed in the ceaseless social chatter.

The central figures in the novel are the Lloberola family, a noble line beginning its decline into failure and impoverishment. The family's regard for social conventions and the hierarchies of social life are matched only by their idleness and their capacity for self-delusion. Against a cultural background dominated by debate about building an ideal, classical city, Sagarra exposes the reality of a perverse, disloyal community of hypocrites and self-servers:

> Outward morality was so fastidious in these families that often it was considered scandalous merely to drop the name of a famous actress or dancer, or intelligent author, or the title of a novel [. . . But] moral rigidity, strictly external, was no impediment in the heart of the most prim and proper families to the basest imaginable sexual practices, cases of vile degeneration.

The first member of the family we meet is Federic Lloberola, one of the two sons of the head of the family Don Tomás. Federic's father 'had seen all the family's grandeur melt in his hands until he had become a poor, grey, defenseless man in a massive, unimportant, practically anonymous residence amid the uniform geometry of Barcelona apartment buildings'. Federic is introduced to the reader as he leaves the bed of his lover, Rosa Trenor, one of a cast of secondary characters who depend on, or exploit, Lloberola family members. Federic's brother Guillem is a waster, a handsome young man with neither vocation nor enthusiasm for anything other than sex and parties. We meet him as he becomes involved in a curious sexual triangle with a wealthy banker and his beautiful young wife, a tryst organised for them by a seamstress who will later, and mysteriously, meet a violent end. Federic himself is a listless, frustrated aristocrat given to alternating bouts of melancholy and arrogant pride in his family background – but above all he is cold and egotistical, the embodiment of the long decline of the Lloberolas.

It seems appropriate that this first part of the novel, set in 1927, should end with a collective trawl by this group of social gadflies through the brothels and cabarets of the Raval, where they watch a sex show with studied indifference, as if they were above it all rather than hopelessly stuck in this corrupt expression of their own decline. In the midst of one of their social gatherings, Primo de Rivera himself, 'a cross between a police inspector and a canasta player, with a touch of the priest and a touch of the lion tamer', appears, to the delight of the ladies present. The Primo dictatorship, Sagarra writes later in the book, 'filled shrivelled stomachs with crusts of bread and offered up a bit of fireworks to cast a reflex of happiness on their curious faces. Cowardice and stupidity on all sides contributed to the game, and yet it cannot be denied that Barcelona did have a brilliant, stupendously decorative moment.' But then the stock market trembled, the crash arrived and the monarch 'gave Primo a kick in the belly'. The fall of the monarch himself would follow soon after.

Pride Before the Fall

By 1930, the supercilious partygoers of Sagarra's novel shared with much of their class a disillusionment with Primo de Rivera. The 1929 Exposition had been a golden opportunity for ostentatious display, but it had ended by bankrupting the city just before the impact of the October crash in the world economy began to take its toll. Primo's dictatorship had invested heavily in construction, especially in the grand project for the exhibition, and the Catalan moneyed classes had speculated wildly on the construction industry and made a killing. The Barcelona regional government was left with an enormous debt, much of it incurred through corrupt dealings and as a result of systematic overcharging.

The second part of the novel is set in 1932, the year of its publication. Primo de Rivera is dead (he died in Paris just months after his fall), and dictatorship has been replaced by the elected government of the Republic. The 1929 Exposition had generated a collective hysteria. 'Barcelona had forgotten all about the days of politics, pistols and bombs,' Sagarra confidently asserts. He would prove to be profoundly mistaken within four years of the novel's publication, but among the circles he had fictionalised, this was almost certainly true. The death of Don Tomás marked the end of the Lloberola inheritance – not biologically, since Guillem and Federic and his children remained – but in the demise of the world in which the name had any kind of meaning. For the ladies of Hortensia Portella's circle of gossips and whisperers, 'all the changes, which were considerable, were viewed as spectacle.' Sagarra's narrative now becomes the collective whispering of the same circles that we had initially encountered under the dictatorship of Primo. Their targets were different, their social lives conducted with some new recruits and in hitherto unacceptable places, but with the same cynicism: 'Ladies of a more conciliatory spirit, some of them the former clientele of the dictator's appetite, went over to the republic. Under the pretext of concerts, art exhibits, charitable balls and cozier, more private parties, the snobberies of old were thrust together with the new.'

Private Life is a panoramic mural of Barcelona's high society, many of whose actual members appear in the novel barely if not at all disguised. Sagarra's prose is scathing, his occasional psychological insights painfully amusing. He is a kind of Noel Coward in his venomous asides, and his detailed social observations are sharp. It is true that he seems at times to be carried away in his own elaborate metaphors, but as a collective portrait of one class of Barcelona's society it is revealing. It is an entertaining but curious mix of insight, satire and gossip, and a vibrant vision of a city whose coming crisis is sensed rather than understood. An old Barcelona was ending, a new city was emerging which would sweep aside not only much of the previous order, but also some of those who had imagined themselves impregnable to change. Still others, of course, would simply change their dress, stop speaking Catalan, and wait.

There was a larger structural problem too. The government of Cataluña was dominated by the most conservative sector of the local bourgeoisie, represented by the Lliga Regionalista whose leader, Francesc Cambó, was violently opposed to Catalan independence in any form. On the other hand, he was an enthusiastic ally of Madrid, despite the fact that Madrid's lack of interest in industrial development or economic modernisation had a double effect on Cataluña: on the one hand it meant that the domestic market for Catalan products remained very limited, while on the other Spain's most profitable and advanced industrial sector was a major contributor to the exchequer of the central state. But Cambó and the people he represented were prepared to accept these constraints in exchange for the presence of Spanish military power. The spectre of the 1919 general strike still haunted them, and their retaliation had begun before that iconic year ended with the three-month lockout by factory owners and the violence that followed.

In 1923, after three years of armed confrontations that claimed the lives of nearly 190 workers and some 21 employers, the tension in the city was undiminished. Cambó and the Lliga, therefore, had welcomed Primo de Rivera's military dictatorship, despite his suppression of all things Catalan, from the printed language to the national dance, the *sardana*. Primo was ferociously hostile to Catalan independence. Within two years he had banned the use of Catalan in schools, churches and in commercial transactions. The Catalan flag was removed from official buildings, the Orfeo Catala was no longer allowed to perform, and even Barcelona Football Club was suspended for six months after fans booed and whistled during the playing of the Royal March. More significantly, the so-called Sindicatos Libres, the Free Unions which were effectively a paramilitary strike-breaking force organising systematic assaults on workers' organisations, were given free rein. At the same time Primo created public works to provide employment in what was a gathering economic crisis – though they were financed by private investment and inflation eroded any advance in living standards that new jobs might have brought. Central to his plans was the organisation of the new International Exposition in 1929, to be held in Barcelona.

First planned by the Modernista Puig i Cadafalch in 1915, the 1929 Exposition was intended to be the expression of Spain's prosperity and progress. It was to be a consciously Spanish affair, with nothing in its construction to acknowledge Cataluña as an autonomous principality. This was, of course, consistent with Primo's prohibition of any expression of Catalan culture. What he had not anticipated was that this grandiose project would coincide with a worldwide economic crisis which had already affected the Catalan and Spanish economies. More importantly, the crash inhibited foreign attendance – and the consequence was an enormous financial loss. The Plaza de España was the entry point to the exhibition, its gateway marked by twin bell towers in the style of those in St Mark's Square in Venice. The dramatic Avenue of Maria Cristina rose in a series of stairways and terraces towards the National Palace at the top, built in the neo-Gothic style favoured by *noucentrisme*. It could not have been further from the creative, impulsive eclecticism of the Modernisme that had dominated Barcelona less than 20 years before. Behind the palace rose the hill of Montjuich.

Montjuich has made several appearances in the history of Barcelona, but always as a military site from which cannon-shot rained down upon the city from time to time. It was also the main prison and the execution site for many activists and mass leaders after the demolition of the Ciutadella, many of whom were buried in the Fosser de la Pedrera, the Quarry Graveyard, behind the castle. It would play that same sombre role for many years thereafter, during and after the Civil War – as a recent monument to the victims in the cemetery testifies today. The 1929 Exposition marked the full integration of Montjuich into the city, at least administratively if not architecturally. The castle overlooks the port still, if with less aggressive intent – it is now a military museum – with the emblematic cable car linking the port to the hill.

The National Palace is now the National Museum of Art redesigned for the 1992 Olympics and accessed by dramatic outside escalators. The museum's collection of Catalan art through the centuries, and especially the religious murals transferred intact to the building's interior, has no rival. Nearby, the Pueblo Español gathers in a single imaginary village the styles of each of Spain's regions. Since the exhibition deliberately ignored any reference to Cataluña it is difficult to see beyond the pueblo's ideological intent and its inescapably kitsch style. Robert Hughes cruelly describes it in *Barcelona* as 'Españolandia'. But the gardens rising up the hill and the beautifully located Teatre Grec provide some continuity and dignity to the whole complex. Among the pavilions in the original 1929 Exposition was a German pavilion, an iconic Modernist building by Mies van der Rohe. Subsequently demolished, it has since been rebuilt and makes a dramatic contrast with the National Museum above it. Further up the hill, reached either through Forestier's restful gardens or direct by funicular, is the Joan Miró Foundation, designed by Josep Maria Sert. It is full of light and air and glorious open views across the port of Barcelona which provide stunning backdrops for some of Miró's sculptures.

Primo de Rivera finally left power in January 1930, having lost the support of the army and the monarchy. His model of control had been corporate and authoritarian, with the National Assembly having only an advisory role. His model of labour relations – control through committees of employers and labour and the banning of strikes – had won over the Unión General de Trabajadores (UGT), the Socialist Party's trade union federation, but only deepened the enmity of the anarchist organisations which had been made illegal and the target of his repressive apparatus. The spiralling economic crisis, meanwhile, led three months later, in April, to the abdication of the king, Alfonso XIII.

In *Private Life*, Sagarra leaves us in no doubt as to the lifestyle of the new bourgeoisie, and their general indolence and disinterest in matters commercial. The years of repression under Primo made little impact on their social lives. And in Mendoza's *City of Marvels*, the enormously powerful and successful Onofre Bouvila, the novel's central character, is an unscrupulous speculator, a gangster capitalist if ever there was one. He may describe himself as 'a flaw in the system', but he seems on the contrary to be an authentic representative of the leading figures in Cataluña's economy at the time. Onofre's spectacular exit at the end of the novel, just as the 1929 Exposition was inaugurated, suggests the ending of an era in which, despite his origins, he had been able to devote himself unchallenged to the pursuit of his personal ambitions for money and power.

The city he left behind was deeply divided. The wealthy and the poor lived physically close to one another, yet the poor only appear tangentially in *Private Life*, as objects of a kind of anthropological curiosity. The distance was reflected in the fearful visions of the poor districts as dangerous places rife with drugs and prostitution, a dark world of criminality and vice. That is what both repelled and fascinated the characters of Sagarra's novel.

By 1930, Barcelona's population had swollen to 1 million. The increase was largely explained by the migration of workers to the industries and construction projects that required the unskilled labour of those arriving from rural poverty in Murcia and Andalucia. The tensions of the early 1920s could have been addressed with social welfare reforms, but instead the complaints of the people were answered with more repression. Education remained in the hands of a deeply conservative Catholic Church, which offered only a tiny proportion of the places needed even under the grim conditions that prevailed in its schools. Public health remained terrible in the narrow streets of the old city, where cholera and typhus were regular visitors. Housing was a major problem, and tiny rooms occupied by several families were commonplace. After the wartime boom, the number of jobs fell, but there were no benefits available to the unemployed, who faced unscrupulous rack rent landlords. The new arrivals, when they did not squeeze into the already overcrowded Raval and Barceloneta, occupied the shanties (*barraques*) beneath the castle on Montjuich or were sent to the cheap housing schemes (*cases barates*) built on wasteland on the outskirts or in some cases close to the factories where there was work.

In these conditions, and where trade unions were illegal, the anarchist CNT grew at dramatic speed. By 1930, its membership nationally was over 750,000, with 250,000 in Barcelona alone. There was no comparable anarchist presence anywhere else in Europe. Whereas the anarchist circles in the period of the '*pistolero* wars' of the early 1920s were dominated by armed self-defence groups, under the Primo dictatorship the CNT increasingly became the expression of community solidarity and shared experience, as well as providing what society at large did not offer – education, organised self-help and cooperation, and cultural possibilities through the Ateneus, which offered schooling along the rationalist lines advocated by Francisco Ferrer's Modern School, lending libraries, musical events and political discussion. Anarchism was deeply suspicious of governments and states, and unlike the Spanish Socialists made no attempt to participate in formal politics.

The population of the Raval would be central actors in the imminent Civil War and would pay a heavy price for their participation. But the area would remain symbolically and socially important, and would attract welcome and unwelcome attention in equal measure in the years to come.

6

CIVIL WAR

Four years after Genet visited Barcelona, and explored its lower depths, Barcelona again played host to a range of visitors from abroad. Their purpose was very different. Many were athletes who had come to take part in the People's Olympiad of 1936, and to see for themselves the new Republic whose Popular Front government had been elected in February 1936.

It was the year of the infamous Berlin Olympics, filmed by Leni Riefenstahl to represent the triumph of Nazism in Germany. To Hitler's fury, the most successful participant was Jesse Owens, the black American athlete who won four gold medals, which Hitler refused to present. Josep Maria de Sagarra, who wrote the Barcelona Olympiad's anthem (with music by Brecht's collaborator Hans Eisler), described the alternative Games as a 'peace festival'. Six thousand athletes assembled in Barcelona for the events, which were scheduled to begin on 19 July. The opening event, on the eve of the inauguration, was to be a concert at which the great Catalan cellist, Pau Casals, would perform.

The Games never took place. On the day before, 18 July, a military rebellion against the Republican government began in Spanish Morocco. It was led by a military junta which included the Chief of Staff of the right-wing CEDA-led government (1934–5), Francisco Franco. Franco would emerge as the leader of the Confederación Española de Derechas Autónomas (CEDA, the Spanish Confederation of Autonomous Right-Wing Groups) a few months later. It was assumed by the leaders of the military coup that there would be little or no resistance to the army, bolstered by Moorish troops, when they launched their military rising in mainland Spain. In fact, what began that day was a civil war that would last for three years.

The Spanish Civil War has been described, misguidedly in my view, as a 'writers' war'. It was in the first instance a social revolution in which two clearly defined political projects confronted one another – the one fascist, and in line with the regimes already established in Germany and Italy when it began in 1936, and the other democratic and anti-fascist, and within it a deeper struggle for a new and different kind of society. Against the background of the rise of Nazism and Italian fascism, Spain was a testing ground. The opposition's hope was that fascism could be halted in its tracks there and the reactionary tide stemmed and turned back. That was certainly how it was seen by many progressive people around the world, such as those who were attending the People's Olympiad. Some 200 of the athletes stayed to defend the Republic against the military rebellion. They were the first of 30,000 foreign volunteers who went to Spain to fight fascism as members of the International Brigades. They included writers, journalists and artists, but the majority were working-class people who made the difficult and dangerous journey to the battlefields from Europe and beyond. Some died there, like the British poets John Cornford and Christopher Caudwell, and others whose names are not as well known.

Of the volunteers who joined, George Orwell is probably among the best remembered, but there were many others, like the group of poets who had met at Oxford University, and who were sympathetic to the Communist cause, including Stephen Spender, Louis MacNeice, Cecil Day-Lewis and W. H. Auden. The poetry of this generation is included in Valentine Cunningham's excellent anthologies, *The Penguin Book of Spanish Civil War Verse* (1980) and *Spanish Front* (1986). Their reasons were expressed with extraordinary intensity by Auden in his poem 'Spain':

What's your proposal? To build the just city? I will.
I agree. Or is it the suicide pact, the romantic
Death? Very well, I accept, for
I am your choice, your decision. Yes, I am Spain.
[. . .]

Tomorrow for the young the poets exploding like bombs,
The walks by the lake, the weeks of perfect communion;
Tomorrow the bicycle races
Through the suburbs on summer evenings.
But today the struggle.
[. . .]

Today the makeshift consolations: the shared cigarette,
The cards in the candlelit barn, and the scraping concert,
The masculine jokes; today the
Fumbled and unsatisfactory embrace before hurting.

The stars are dead. The animals will not look.
We are left alone with our day, and the time is short, and
History to the defeated
May say Alas but cannot help nor pardon.

In later years Auden distanced himself from the feelings he
expressed there, claiming that they were misguided. It seems more
likely that he was embarrassed by his radicalism at that time. But
the poem exists, is extremely powerful, and represents the feelings of
Auden and others at the moment that the Civil War began. Stephen
Spender also reviewed his involvement with hindsight. Having
attended the International Cultural Congress in April 1937 in
Valencia, and joined the Communist Party, Spender later criticised
what he saw as the dogmatism and dishonesty of the Communist
organisers of the Brigades. Yet many people saw Spain as Auden

did at the time, as a historic crossroads where a bright future was threatened by barbaric and backward forces.

Preludes to War

The municipal elections of 12 April 1931 in Cataluña produced an extraordinary result. The Republican Esquerra Republicana de Catalunya (ERC, Catalan Republican Left) and its allies won 38 of the 50 seats in the Barcelona City Council. In Madrid, the parties who some months earlier had signed the Pact of San Sebastian, a coalition that included Republicans, Socialists and the Radicals, led by the Catalan populist Alejandro Lerroux, formed the new Republican government. The monarchy was no more, and Alfonso XIII and his mother departed in haste and without fanfare.

Two days later, on 14 April, Francesc Macià, 'l'Avi' ('Grandfather'), leader of the ERC, stood on the balcony of the Generalitat in Plaza Sant Jaume, to announce to a large crowd the formation of the Catalan Republic within a federal Spain. Macià was a military officer who had resigned his commission in protest at the treatment of the Catalans; in 1926 he had led an attempted invasion of Cataluña from France, which was stopped at the border. Subirachs's monument to him stands today in one corner of the Plaza Catalunya, near the start of the Ramblas, an upside-down stairway that represents the progress of Cataluña. Macià's party manifesto promised a programme of social welfare, accessible housing (*la caseta i l'hortet* – a little house and garden), and the refusal to pay the extravagant debts corruptly incurred by the government to finance the 1929 Exposition. The packed square received his announcement with delirium. And although the CNT had abstained from the election campaign on principle, and had not openly supported the ERC, a significant proportion of the cheering crowd were certainly its members. Whatever its misgivings, the CNT saw the advantages of being able to operate legally again. The celebration was short lived. Within 24 hours, the finance minister of the Madrid government, Indalecio Prieto, a Socialist, had forced Macià to accept and pay the debts by freezing state funds to Cataluña, and insisted that his declaration of the Catalan republic be withdrawn in favour of a statute of autonomy, which led to the first regional government, the Generalitat.

In Cataluña and beyond, conservative Spain gathered its forces to resist the reforms proposed by the Republican government. The Church mobilised against education reform, landlords refused to countenance land redistribution, and the organs of repression still threatened the street-level movements. There were contradictions within Cataluña too. Some Catalans were openly hostile to outsiders, for example, and saw the solution to unemployment and the housing shortage in simple, racist terms. Remove the 35 per cent of Barcelona's population who were non-Catalans! A train was even provided to take them back to Murcia in 1931, with ample food and drink on board. On the appointed day the train was packed, but before it left Tarrassa, outside Barcelona, the train was forced to stop and its passengers left for their nearby homes, taking the food and drink with them.

More serious unresolved tensions produced confrontations throughout 1932. The Catalan statute was finally passed by the Madrid parliament, but it was a retreat from Macià's original plan. New laws of social control passed by Madrid early in 1933, and the announcement that the new regime would be a 'Republic of Order', fired a clear warning shot at Cataluña and the CNT in particular. As internal disagreements made the situation increasingly untenable, Spanish-wide elections were called for November 1933. The new government was dominated by the right and included the CEDA, the far-right Catholic party led by José Maria Gil Robles which was pledged to withdraw all the advances achieved or planned under the Republican government of Manuel Azaña. It withdrew the Catalan statute. Macià died at Christmas 1933, and when Lluis Companys, now the leader of the ERC, declared the Estat Catalá, the Catalan state, in the context of widespread agitation against the far right, the Generalitat was closed down and Companys imprisoned.

The subsequent two years, 1934–5, are known as *el bienio negro* (the two black years). It was a period of institutional violence and moments of heroic resistance, such as the Asturias miners' strike, which was crushed by largely North African troops commanded by Colonel Francisco Franco. In January 1936 the Popular Front, which was essentially an alliance of the left Republican, Socialist and Communist parties, presented its programme in the elections of February. The anarchists did not join the pact, but nevertheless, in February 1936, the Popular Front won the elections and moved to form a government.

In Barcelona, the response to the election was immediate. Political prisoners were released as demonstrators converged on the jails, demanding their release, including that of Lluis Companys. The Generalitat was restored. The city, and Cataluña, had lived through two years in which Catalan rights were suppressed and measures for social change reversed. In a highly politicised city where tens of thousands of people were members of the CNT and other left organisations, the frustrated hopes of previous years made themselves felt in a growing polarisation.

It was common knowledge that the right-wing parties, having lost the elections, would look for ways to bring the new government down. They immediately threw their weight behind the coup which was declared on 18 July. The coup leaders had already forged alliances with Hitler and Mussolini to assist them. Although the government had been democratically elected, its Western European allies were less than enthusiastic about defending a government of the left – all the more so when Communists entered the government in November. The reaction of much of Europe soon after the Civil War began was to form a non-intervention committee which, paradoxically, included Germany and Italy, who nevertheless supplied the rebels with massive military assistance throughout the subsequent three years.

Rebellion!

The military coup of 18 July lifted the lid on the tensions beneath. Barcelona was clearly a key part of the insurgents' plan, not least because of the strength of the popular forces there. The city was to be taken by soldiers from the barracks around the city, under the command of General Goded, who travelled to the city from Mallorca.

André Malraux, the future French Resistance fighter and minister, volunteered as a pilot for the Republic. His 1937 novel, *L'Espoir* (*Days of Hope*), is among the most profound representations of the Civil War as it unfolds across Spain. It begins in Barcelona, on the day of the military rebellion:

> A factory whistle shrieked through the morning air. As on the days when only trivial destinies are in the making; as on the workdays when the Negus and his friends had heard the whistles calling and hurried to their work, along grey and yellow walls, walls without end; in the same flush of dawn, with the same street-lamps still alight, seeming to dangle from the trolley wires [. . .] Another siren hooted. Ten, twenty sirens. A hundred!
>
> All stopped dead in the middle of the road, struck dumb with wonder. Never had any of them heard more than five sirens going at once. As in Spanish cities of old when all the belfries jangled a summons to the townsfolk in the hour of peril, so now the proletariat of Barcelona answered the volleys with the tocsin of their factory whistles.

The battles between the rebel troops and the local militia and armed workers, as well as, to everyone's astonishment, a battalion of the hated Civil Guard, raged through the day, centred on Plaza Catalunya. By evening the rebellion was defeated. 'A ruddy glow spread up the sky beyond the square [. . .] Then on every hand, wisps of bright red fire began to flicker above the house-tops.

That morning Barcelona had summoned the whole city with the shriek of her sirens. Now by night she was sending her churches up in flames.'

Ronald Fraser's wonderful oral history of the Civil War, *Blood of Spain* (1994), is a kind of choral work, the events retold through the experience of some 600 participants telling their own stories:

> Miquel Coll, a POUM textile worker [. . .] ran towards the Ramblas; on the corner of the Carrer Ferran he saw that Beristain, a sports and gun shop, was being ransacked for arms. He rushed in and grabbed a shotgun. A CNT man broke open the safe and pulled out wads of banknotes.
>
> Then he struck a match and set fire to the lot. He burnt every note. It was amazing – true proof of the honour that so many CNT militants like him displayed. I grabbed two bandoliers and strapped them across my chest, stuffed full of cartridges, and went out of there looking like one of those Mexican bandits you see in films. I was only twenty.

By 19 July, the military barracks were surrounded and the troops prevented from marching by the massive mobilisation of CNT members and others. Goded was arrested and detained with others on the prison ship *Uruguay* in the harbour. (That he got there unharmed was thanks to the intervention of Caridad Mercader, a Communist Party member and the mother of the man who later murdered Leon Trotsky in Mexico.) He later surrendered in a radio broadcast: 'This is General Goded speaking. I want to let everybody know that the day has gone against me. I am a prisoner. I make this known so that those who do not wish to keep up the struggle may know that they are absolved of any obligation towards me.'

The anti-fascist militias who defeated the coup attempt in Barcelona later moved to the Aragon front to stop the advance on the city from the west. The situation there is powerfully and movingly depicted in Ken Loach's film *Land and Freedom* (1995). The issue now was the attitude of the anarchists towards the government of Companys; he was well known to them, having defended a number of anarchists as a lawyer before the war. In September, Companys invited the anti-fascist militias to join his government. The CNT was bitterly divided about whether or not to accept, but three leading members did join the cabinet, together with Andreu Nin, the leader of the small but influential organisation of anti-Stalinist revolutionaries, the POUM, with whose militia Orwell fought on the Aragon front.

Those who were responsible for the *bienio negro* were now pursued, although Cambó, leader of the conservative Lliga Regionalista, escaped. The atmosphere in Barcelona was of excitement and optimism. The city came under the control of the mass organisations and the trade unions. Langdon-Davies describes, in his *Behind the Spanish Barricades*, a visit to the Ritz, once the exclusive province of the very rich (as it is once again today) but now taken over by the waiters' union, where queues of people from the Raval formed outside the restaurant, waiting to be fed: 'In Barcelona the Ritz was used by the CNT and the UGT as "Gastronomic Unit Number One" – a public canteen for all those in need [. . .] Everyone who went was supposed to have a pass from his local committee, but the guards "refused to be bureaucratic".'Not only did few people attempt to eat twice but, according to Langdon-Davies, little of the Ritz cutlery disappeared. The anarchists ascribed this to the fact that it now belonged neither to a private concern nor to the state – the people did not steal from themselves. The basic principle was that the community should take on all responsibility for welfare. To leave it to the state was to give authoritarianism a human face. Public safety, too, was now the province of the grassroots organisations; factories were placed under the control of workers' committees and the militia controlled the streets.

George Orwell arrived in Barcelona in November, and later fought at the Battle of Huesca on the Aragon front. It is his account of the early phase of the Civil War in Barcelona, *Homage to Catalonia* (1938), which has become its best-known testimony in the English-speaking world. Ironically, it was John Langdon-Davies' *Behind the Spanish Barricades* which was the greater commercial success at the time. In fact, Orwell's independent political position, and his criticism of Stalinism, blocked the publication of his book for nearly nine years, and it was only after the publication of his *1984* that *Homage to Catalonia* won its place as a key account of the war in Barcelona with this, very famous, passage:

> I had come to Spain with some notion of writing newspaper articles, but I had joined the militia almost immediately, because at that time and in that atmosphere it seemed the only conceivable thing to do. The Anarchists were still in virtual control of Catalonia and the revolution was still in full swing. To anyone who had been there since the beginning it probably seemed even in December or January [1937] that the revolutionary period was ending; but when one came straight from England the aspect of Barcelona was something startling and overwhelming. It was the first time that I had ever been in a town where the working class was in the saddle [. . .] Every shop and cafe had an inscription saying that it had been collectivized; even the bootblacks had been collectivized and their boxes painted red and black. Waiters and shop-walkers looked you in the face and treated you as an equal. Servile and even ceremonial forms of speech had temporarily disappeared. Nobody said 'Señor' or 'Don' or even 'Usted'; everyone called everyone else 'Comrade' and 'Thou', and said 'Salud!' instead of 'Buenos dias'. Tipping was forbidden by law.

Langdon-Davies had spent many years in Cataluña, and returned in 1936 as a correspondent of the *News Chronicle*. His account of the war there was therefore based on a more detailed knowledge. His political position was less radical than Orwell's; as he explained to an inquisitive anarchist official when he arrived in Barcelona:

'I am neither Stalinite nor Trotskyite. In fact I am nothing much.' Yet his description of the city, in August, echoes Orwell's:

> The Ramblas lie sloping gradually upward for more than a mile to the Plaça de Catalunya. From the other end you look down on an unending harvest of heads. Today there is not a hat, a collar, or a tie to be seen among them, the sartorial symbols of the bourgeoisie are gone, a proletarian freedom has swarmed in along the Calle del Hospital and the Calle del Carmen from the Parallel. Or as Puig suggests, the bourgeoisie have disguised themselves as proletarians by leaving hat, collar and tie at home.

As Orwell describes it, those symbols of respectability would reappear the following year, but for the moment Barcelona was in the full flow of a social revolution. His impressions are echoed by Franz Borkenau, whose *The Spanish Cockpit* (1937) is one of the best accounts of the Spanish Civil War:

> Now when I went out the streets were full of excited groups of young men in arms, and not a few armed women as well, the latter behaving with a self-assurance unusual for Spanish women when they appear in public (and it would be unthinkable before for a Spanish girl to appear in trousers, as the militia-girls invariably do) but with decency. Particularly numerous groups gathered before the fashionable buildings now requisitioned as party centres. The enormous Hotel Colon, dominating the splendid Plaza de Cataluña has been taken over by the PSUC [Catalan Communist Party]. The anarchists with an eye for striking contrasts have expropriated the offices of the Fomento de Trabajo [the employers' organisation], in the fashionable Layetana. The Trotskyists have settled down in the Hotel Falcón, on the Ramblas.

Orwell famously found himself at the Hotel Falcón on the Ramblas, and today the Plaza George Orwell sits beside it. The

9 The Plaza George Orwell off the Ramblas

hotel itself is now the Fundación Andreu Nin, named in honour of the revolutionary socialist who led the POUM and was killed by communist agents in 1937. Borkenau travelled to Barcelona in August 1937 in the company of John Cornford, a young British poet who died in battle on the Huesca front.

Like Orwell, Borkenau noted how the atmosphere in the city had changed by the end of that year:

The Ramblas, the chief artery of popular life in Barcelona, were far less working class now than then. In August it was dangerous to wear a hat; nobody minded doing so now, and the girls no longer hesitated to wear their prettiest clothes. A few of the more fashionable restaurants and dancehalls have reopened, and find customers [. . .] The Hotel Continental, where I had stayed in August, one of the few journalists among a large crowd of billeted militia, had entirely resumed its pre-revolutionary aspect. The militia had been removed, the rooms were full of paying and fairly well-dressed guests, and business in this particular hotel seemed to be excellent.

Within Barcelona, for the first year of the war, the battle developed on two linked fronts – the war against the fascist forces under Franco was conducted on the Aragon front which remained the outer perimeter of the war on Cataluña until early 1938. In the city the social revolution that the CNT and the POUM had proclaimed involved a deeper transformation, in effect a transfer of power to the grassroots organisations. Control of daily life passed into their hands, as exemplified by the waiters who had taken over the Ritz. This was the dream that so many were willing to fight for, just as Orwell had described it. But there was a second conflict going on within the Republic itself. The Western powers, Britain and France in particular,

10 *A Republican fighter during the Civil War*

had withdrawn their support for the Republic, proclaiming instead their 'non-intervention', as if it were simply a local matter. The visible presence of the German and Italian military fighting with Franco was simply ignored. Yet the government of the Republic was properly elected. For Britain and France, the main consideration was to avoid being drawn into war with Germany, and to avoid compromises with a government which was supported by Communists – where they saw the hidden hand of Stalin.

Events came to a head in May 1937 around the Telefónica building in the corner of the Plaza Catalunya, which still belongs to the now-multinational Spanish telecommunications company. The building was controlled by the anarchist trade unions, and the government complained that union members listened in to, and occasionally interrupted, ministerial calls to the government in Madrid. The real question, of course, was who controlled the city? After four days the armed confrontation was ended by the CNT leaders, over the objections of their revolutionary allies in the POUM. One of them, Wildebaldo Solano, described the moment to Ronald Fraser:

> They refused to reach agreement. As we got up to leave one of them [the CNT leaders] patted us on the shoulder and said 'It's been a pleasant evening together.' I'll never forget it as long as I live. I'd crossed the city from barricade to barricade twice in a few hours simply to be told what a pleasant evening we'd had.

The government-controlled Guardia de Asalto, Assault Guards, took the building. Many of those inside were arrested and some leading members of the left organisations were later murdered, most famously Andreu Nin, leader of the POUM. Their assassins, however, were members of the Communist Party, supposedly their allies in the defence of the Republic. The objective was to crush the revolutionary forces and demonstrate to the Western governments that this was not a revolution, but the defence of a democratic government and nothing more.

The debate around these issues, and especially the significance of those days in May, has produced a vast literature, arguing the case for both sides. Malraux addressed it in his novel *Days of Hope*, as did John Langdon-Davies and many others. It is also explored in the fine novel about the murder of Trotsky by the Cuban writer, Leonardo Padura Fuentes, *The Man who Loved Dogs* (2009) where Cataluña and the Spanish Civil War figure large.

Barcelona was always the ultimate prize for the fascists. The final entry of Franco's forces into the city came on 26 January 1939. By then the city had undergone sustained bombardment, first from an Italian warship in the harbour in February 1937. Aerial bombardment began in January 1938 and continued through most of the year, claiming over 2,500 victims. It was the first sustained bombing of a major city since the day-long destruction of Guernica a year earlier. Martha Gellhorn, the American journalist, was in the city with Ernest Hemingway when it began. Her biographer, Caroline Moorhead, writes in *Gellhorn: A Twentieth-Century Life* (2004): 'The loyalist tropos were forced to retreat and Martha and Hemingway followed the line of smashed and abandoned trucks, taking shelter behind low stone walls to watch the fascist bombers "high and bright like dragonflies" glinting in the sun high above. When they came in to drop their loads, they made an echo that circled round the mountains.'

The American poet Langston Hughes was also present during one of the raids, as he recalled in his poem 'Air Raid Barcelona':

> The death birds wheel East
> To their lairs again
> Leaving iron eggs
> [. . .]
> A child weeps alone
> Men uncover bodies
> From ruins of stone.

The bombs were carefully targeted, the majority falling on Barceloneta, with its factories, and on the Raval. In early February a column of 80,000 refugees escaping the city made their way to the French frontier (in all, 400,000 people crossed the border).They crossed into Vichy France, a Nazi ally not well disposed to the Republican and anti-fascist refugees. Many were held in concentration camps in southern France and later set to work in German factories. In small towns around the south, and particularly the Catalan-speaking Rousillon, it is not uncommon to find plaques commemorating the role Spaniards and Catalans played in the French Resistance.

The Spanish Civil War, as is now very clear, was a wider international conflict played out on Spanish soil. The fascist forces led by Franco included German and Italian armament and troops – 70,000 of the latter. It was German planes that bombed the Basque town of Guernica, and Italian planes that strafed the streets of Barcelona in 1937 and 1938. On the Republican side, by contrast, there was aid from Russia, but that aid was tied to political limitations on the government as Stalin and the Soviets tried, without success, to convince the so-called non-interventionist nations of their commitment to bourgeois democracy. Beyond that, direct solidarity came from the International Brigades, whose 35,000 members were for the most part working-class people moved by the news from Spain. Ethel Macdonald, a young woman from Glasgow who broadcast on anarchist radio stations from Barcelona was one; another, a young engineering apprentice from the same city, Alex McDade, was killed at the Battle of Brunete in 1938. He left an enduring legacy in his rewritten lyrics to the old American tune 'Red River Valley'. It is included by Valentine Cunningham in his *Anthology of Spanish Civil War Poetry* (1980):

> There's a valley in Spain called Jarama
> It's a place that we all know so well
> For it's there that we wasted our manhood
> And most of our old age as well.

> From this valley they tell us we're leaving
> But don't hasten to bid us adieu
> For e'en though we make our departure
> We'll be back in an hour or two.

The Spanish Civil War continued to fascinate and absorb writers and artists long after the destruction of the Republic. The bibliography is huge, though the literature is overwhelmingly testimonial. And the debate about what was possible, what was won and what lost, and who was responsible for its outcome, remains alive and intense today. In Spain itself, the experience of war remained a hidden history for many years. Companys was shot in 1940, and his tomb, together with many others – the anarchist leaders José Ascaso and Buenaventura Durruti (both killed in 1936), as well as Francisco Ferrer, the educationalist executed in 1909 – are to be found in Fossar de les Pedreres on Montjuich, where so many were shot by the Franco forces after the war, or in La Bota, the execution site in the Barceloneta.

For Whom the Bell Tolls

The title of Ernest Hemingway's hugely successful 1940 novel and its fine film version by Sam Wood, starring Gary Cooper and Ingrid Bergman, says a great deal about the international impact of the Spanish Civil War. For many people, it had become much more than a local conflict; it was the theatre in which democracy and fascism faced one another in a first, unequal confrontation. The military machine of German and Italian fascism overwhelmed a republic whose only external ally, the Soviet Union, was a reluctant friend. Stalin was more interested in winning the approval of the Western powers, especially Britain and France, who had both effectively turned their backs on Spain. Hemingway's title – derived from John Donne's meditation that starts 'No man is an island', with its famous final words: 'And therefore never send to know for whom the bell tolls; it tolls for thee' – makes the powerful point that what was at stake in Spain affected everyone, just as the defeat of the Republic had. If the leaders of the military coup had wrongly assumed the war would last a matter of days, it was because they underestimated the spirit of a popular movement defending its own future. When the character of the war changed, and its spontaneous, grassroots mobilisations were constrained and disciplined by a state under Communist Party domination, that spirit ebbed. It was what Orwell and Borkenau, and many others, had noticed and written about. Hemingway's novel is set during the Civil War. His protagonist, Robert Jordan has come to Spain to join the International Brigades and is working as a dynamiter with a Republican guerrilla group around the town of Segovia.

Laurie Lee was a British volunteer. His book *As I Walked Out One Midsummer Morning* (1969), the sequel to his much-loved

11 *Monument to the International Brigades, Barcelona*

description of a West Country childhood in *Cider with Rosie,* was an account of his travels in Spain with his violin just before the Civil War. He published a further volume about his experiences in Spain in 1992. *A Moment of War* was published over 20 years later and narrates his journey back to Spain in 1937. It is a sensitively written, but perhaps disillusioned account of the drab and humiliating realities of war. In a way it is anti-heroic; most of his experiences after crossing the Pyrenees alone are disappointing – he is arrested, met with suspicion and hostility and jailed in terrible conditions. Much of his time is spent simply waiting:

> But what brought us here anyway? My reasons seemed simple enough, in spite of certain confusions. But so then were those of most of the others – failure, poverty, debt, the law, betrayal by wives or lovers – most of the usual things that sent one to foreign wars. But in our case, I believe, we shared something else, unique to us at that time – the chance to make one grand, uncomplicated gesture of personal sacrifice and faith which might never occur again. Certainly it was the last time that a generation had such an opportunity before the fog of nationalism and mass-slaughter closed in.

In the end, even a war fought for heroic ends can become debilitating and brutal, and all the more so when, as happened in Spain, the idealism that informed the first resistance is undermined by political expediency and sectarianism. When Lee is finally directly involved in battle, it is at the devastating defeat of Teruel, before he reaches Barcelona and is able to return to the border:

> It was then that I began to sense for the first time something of the gaseous squalor of a country at war, an infection so deep it seemed to rot the earth, drain it of colour, life and sound. This was not the battlefield, but acts of war had been committed here, little murders, small excesses of vengeance. The landscape was

plagued, stained and mottled, and all humanity seemed to have been banished from it.

A similar atmosphere pervades the very popular novel by Joan Sales, *Incierta gloria* (*Uncertain Glory*, 1956). It is set on the Aragon front, where Orwell briefly fought and John Cornford was killed, and where the first effective mass defence of the revolution was mounted. The book was initially published in 1956, in a heavily truncated version, and then republished, in full but with changes and additions, between 1971 and 1986. Recently published in English, it is a well-written, often lyrical narrative. Though it is set during the Spanish Civil War it is not, unlike the other largely testimonial accounts, *about* the war; rather the Civil War is the frame within which the novel's cast confront material and existential questions. The central character, Lluis Braco, is sent to the Aragon front, yet the war is largely distant – explosions dimly heard, rumours of fighting, and it is Lluis's infatuation with the *carlana*, the local landowner's wife, that seems central to the fiction. The experiences of war in Aragon come largely through her memories, though she has held herself apart from the local communities, remaining within her grand, if rundown, country house.

Lluis has left behind his partner, Trini, in Barcelona; a friend since student days, Trini is the daughter of an anarchist. They are not married and have a small son, Ramonet. The second section of the novel is a lengthy series of letters between Trini and Juli Soleras, a friend of both, who appears in the first part as a soldier at the front. Juli is generally cynical and dedicated to avoiding action rather than fighting. Every war probably has its Juli, with no clear political position other than a rampant individualism, and no real commitment to either cause. In the second part of the novel it becomes clear, for example, that he is engaged in large-scale black marketeering, as he keeps Trini in milk and potatoes for much of the time. The third part (and a fourth narrative added later, which is not included in the English edition) is narrated in the first person by Cruell, who later becomes a priest and was also in Aragon. Juli seems to belong far more to the existentialist movement of the 1950s, when the book was written and published, than to the period in which the novel is set. His cynicism about ideology sets him apart from the prevailing atmosphere in a war that was ideologically driven. He is often described as Dostoyevskian, in the sense that his motivations are personal and psychological.

The three friends had met at university, distributing the anarchist newspaper *La Barrinada*. They rarely sold any, it would seem, and when they left a pile in the cathedral beside the free religious pamphlets, none was taken. Trini's father is an anarchist, but also a pacifist, a strange animal in a war where the anarchist organisations were the main driving force in the first year of resisting fascism, precisely at the Aragon front. Anarchist actions at the front are represented in a critical light in the novel, as arbitrary and destructive, through the eyes of the *carlana*. Trini's brother is clearly part of the Republican bureaucracy, a careerist with very few scruples and even fewer anarchist principles. We learn in Cruell's account in the third part of the novel that he has become a PR consultant in postwar Barcelona, working with the business community that supported Franco.

In the course of the war in Barcelona, which Trini describes in her letters, her allegiances seem oddly unclear. She moves between social circles, some anarchist, some religious. Juli in the end betrays Lluis's passion for the *carlana* to Trini.

Although the first two parts of Sales's book are set during the war, on the front and in Barcelona, it is a narrative of disillusionment, a questioning of the necessity of war and of the real motives that drive its participants. It reflects on the Civil War from a Barcelona under fascist control. Its narrative voices are those of the defeated, after all. His verdict on their shared experience is disillusioned and sad, an epitaph on the uncertain glory of youth. And in the end the participation of each of the protagonists in the Civil War was accidental, individual and born only of the need to survive:

And the whole of one's youth is simply the uncertain glory of an April morning, a dark storm crossed by flashes of glory. But what glory, my God? Perhaps the worst thing about war is the peace that follows. You wake from your youth as you would after a disturbed and feverish night, but then you remember it, remember that dark storm, as if nothing outside that was of any value. I am just a survivor, a ghost, living on memories alone. It is the long post-war period, the tunnel and the night where 'we floated like driftwood' [. . .] and thought only of surviving at least until the following day.

For the next 40 years, under Franco, the war was spoken of in whispers, or not at all, in the city. The first cautious reflections came in the 1960s, and largely among exiles. Over 70 years later, the Spanish Civil War continues to be a living issue for Catalans and for Spaniards more widely. Under Franco the memory of it was suppressed, and only the official version – that it was a moral crusade – permitted. But it was not forgotten. When democracy returned to Spain after the dictator's death it was inevitable that it would once again be discussed and argued over. The scars were still not healed, and there was no one who was not in some way affected by it. The writers of the post-Franco era returned to it again and again. It was a shared trauma that in one way or another had to be healed. As the twenty-first century began, as we shall see, the campaign for the Recovery of Historical Memory was testimony to its significance and its impact on every succeeding generation.

7

THE WHISPERING CITY

The Fall

By early 1939, the column of refugees at the French border reached 80,000. They were fleeing the bombardment of the city and the anticipated vengeance of the fascist troops. The writer Max Aub was among them. He tried to escape Franco's Spain after the Civil War but was captured and sent to a forced labour camp in Algeria, where he wrote his *Diario de Djelfa* (*Djelfa Diary*, 1944):

> I remember Barcelona
> I remember all of Spain,
> The smallest details
> Stay in my memory [. . .]
> Three years ago yesterday, Barcelona fell.
> Perhaps you will never be again my Barcelona
> The Barcelona that I loved best;
> A little down at heel, broken, hungry,
> Its heart torn out, its windows broken, wounded
> Moth-eaten, hard.
> Perhaps you'll be again the city I knew as a girl
> A little wilful
> A little overbearing
> A little too much of a housewife
> Devoted, perhaps a little too devoted, to her language
> A little too wanting to be Spanish,
> A little too tall

A little too fat
Barcelona, Barcelona, so hurt
You'll never know how much I loved you.
Three years ago today, Barcelona fell.

The bombardment of the city from the air and from the sea began on 16 March 1938. An early victim was Julia Gay, mother of the three Goytisolo brothers, Juan and Luis, both novelists, and José Agustín, the poet, who wrote of her death:

> Where you wouldn't have been
> If one beautiful morning in Barcelona
> In my Barcelona
> Full of birds and flowers and girls
> But suddenly smashed
> By the roar of bombers
> Flown by men
> Who laughed and talked and sang
> In the German language [. . .]
> right here
> where you wouldn't have been
> on that beautiful morning
> if God hadn't forgotten you.

Their mother's death haunted all three brothers, and references to it recur in their work.

The poet Louis MacNeice returned to Barcelona late in 1938 and wrote some of his finest poetry there. He later published his memoir of those times – *Autumn Journal* (1939):

The shops are ghosts of shops, only open in the morning, the counters and shelves bare, one object every two yards. The cafés are ghosts of cafés – no coffee, beer, spirits or wine, people making do with coloured water which is called lemonade or with terribly

degraded vermouth (yet in one there was a string quartet). They
close at nine and the chairs are piled on the tables. But the people
though thin and often ill, are far from being ghosts of people.

Despite everything, he found the people 'courageous, good
humoured and generous'.

But when the fascists were at the gates, almost half the city's
population fled north, to the French border, joining the refugee
columns along the coast roads.

It was a calculated insult by Franco to wait outside the city for two
extra days in order to march in the occupying troops on 26 January
1939 to avenge the defeat of the Spanish armies by the Catalans on that
day in 1641, during the war of the Segadors. Barcelona had already
been bombed from the sea, by Italian battleships, and from the air. As
the troops marched in, 80,000 people were making their way towards
the French border – a column recorded by the great photographer
Robert Capa. In the end some 400,000 crossed the border in flight
from the expected postwar reprisals. The Franco government took
its revenge with particular brutality on the Catalans, in retaliation
for the region's historical defiance and for what in the eyes of the
new regime was the greatest offence – the 'separatism' that called into
question the unity of a Spain ruled from Madrid.

Franco's Revenge

The first actions of the new regime were retaliatory in every
sense. All Catalan institutions were immediately made illegal; the
Generalitat was abolished and Barcelona's status as the capital of
Cataluña removed. All Catalan associations – trade unions, political
organisations and cultural associations – were suppressed and all
public references to the Catalan language prohibited. Castilian
Spanish was not only imposed on schools, public institutions and
the Church in Cataluña, but every street, square or building bearing

a Catalan name was rebaptised. Even the Library of Cataluña was renamed the Central Library.

In October 1940 the president of the Catalan government, Lluís Companys, who had been arrested by the Germans in Belgium and deported back to Cataluña, was executed by firing squad at the Fossar de la Pedrera, on Montjuich. The Catalan stock market – where Gil Foix had lived through his rise and fall in Oller's *Gold Fever* – was closed down, and its financial system taken over by Spanish banks approved by the regime.

Spain's raw materials were now largely exported towards the Franco regime's allies in Germany and Italy, in gratitude for their support during the Civil War. After 1945, Spain became a pariah in the new Europe; its response was economic self-sufficiency, autarky, with its inevitable consequence in scarcity of basic goods and hunger, especially in the countryside. It was a brutal revenge that Franco wreaked upon the dissident nationalities, the Basques and the Catalans. Foreign or domestic companies seeking to open plants or start production there were denied permission, their requests stamped with the message 'Industry authorised only outside the Catalan provinces'.

In the new regime, under Spain's own version of fascism, Falangism, the most conservative of values would prevail. Women would return to the kitchen and to explicit obedience to their husbands under the vigilant eye of the Falange's Feminine Section run by Franco's sister. Schools came under the exclusive control of the Catholic Church.

These years are explored and recounted in what is rightly considered a masterpiece of Catalan literature, *La Plaça del Diamant* (*In Diamond Square*) by Mercè Rodoreda, published in 1962. To describe it in this way, however, belies the lightness of touch and the lyrical intensity of this beautiful novel. It is the story of a young woman, Natalia. She lives in the Gracia district of Barcelona and works as a shop assistant. Gracia was only incorporated into the city in the 1890s – until then it had been an autonomous village, and today, despite the fact that it is a central and sought-after district of the contemporary city, it retains something of the atmosphere of the village it once was. Diamond Square remains, as it was in Rodoreda's youth, a meeting place – especially for the young. The square has been gentrified and updated – and a statue of Colometa now graces it.

Natalia is a young working girl who is fond of dancing and is going out with a young man until she is waylaid at the dance by Quimet, called Joe in the English translation. He is more than a little overbearing, and her innocence and her vulnerability make her an easy target for his combination of pretty promises and pressure.

He immediately renames her, for example, Colometa – or Pidgey, as she appears in the translation. There is a sort of double entendre at the novel's heart, since the Catalan word 'colom' means both dove and pigeon, with their very different associations:

> Nothing in the world [Joe said] could beat the Parc Guell and the Sagrada Familia and the wavy balconies of the Pedrera. I said they were very nice but far too many waves and sharp spikes as far as I was concerned. He tapped my knee with the side of his hand [. . .] and said if I wanted to be his wife I'd have to start liking every single thing he liked.

Pidgey is unassuming and allows herself to be persuaded to marry Joe, who unquestionably dominates much of her early life. At first she defers to him in all sorts of ways, and accepts his opinions about everything. Most significantly, in her symbolic universe, she accepts the pigeons he brings home on an impulse. As they multiply they also begin to take over Pidgey's life, first from their pigeon loft on the roof and then when they are brought into her flat by her children one day when she has left them alone to go to work. The novel evolves into a narrative of Barcelona through the years of the Republic, the Civil War and afterwards. But the strength of the book is that it is recounted and reflected through the eyes and inner

*12 Statue of
Colometa, the
central character
of Rodoreda's* In
Diamond Square, *in
the square itself in the
Gracia district*

thoughts of a young woman who is forced to learn how to survive and accept the responsibilities thrust upon her by circumstance. And as she grows, the prose of her daily life becomes more thoughtful and more poetic. Her husband Joe and his closest friend are sent to the Aragon front, where they are killed. In the meantime, the struggle for survival in a city devoid of even the most basic goods becomes increasingly desperate. Faced with the real possibility of hunger, she accepts her friend Julie's suggestion of taking her son to a camp; but when she arrives it is clear that it is a brutal place, that her son knows it too, but that she has no alternative. The guilt is corrosive: 'We returned to Barcelona as if we'd perpetrated an evil deed. Halfway home it started to rain and the wiper went from one side to the other, swish, swish, swish, and the water streamed down the glass like a river of tears.'

Her personal tragedies are expressed through a poetic language which is at once innocent and intensely moving. She is a woman whose inner voice strengthens her capacity to survive. Her friend Julie describes making love in a wealthy family home left empty during the Civil War:

> I'd have given anything to enjoy a night of love like the one she'd enjoyed, but I had my work cut out cleaning offices [. . .] and looking after my children and all the beautiful things in life like the wind and the creeping ivy and cypresses spearing the air [. . .] weren't meant for me [. . .] I could only look forward to headaches and sadness.

Pidgey is an involuntary participant in the historic events in her city, but she lives them out through a filter of day-to-day survival. If it were a documentary or a realist novel only, *In Diamond Square* might make depressing reading. But Pidgey's inner voice, and her resolution to survive, are intense and lyrical in Rodoreda's narrative, which is never anything other than Pidgey's own voice. Perhaps its most dramatic moment comes when, at the end of her tether, she buys acid to kill her children and herself to put an end to her hunger and sense of hopelessness. She sees herself as a cork, floating aimlessly, but her despair passes and she ends up as the wife of the grocer on the corner, who thanks her for the joy she has brought him. It is enough. And her final thoughts travel through a universe of impressions, memories, momentary encounters: 'I thought how that afternoon when I went to the park as usual, I might still find puddles on the side paths [. . .] and inside each puddle, however small, there would be a sky [. . .] a sky a bird sometimes disturbed [. . .] a thirsty bird disturbing the sky unawares with water in its beak.'

Rodoreda herself is a fascinating figure. Born in 1908 to working parents in the Sant Gervasi district, she married her uncle, 17 years her senior, when she was still very young. They had one son, but it was clearly not a happy marriage. Rodoreda began writing stories and with the advent of the Republic began to contribute political and cultural articles to a number of Catalan publications. In

13 *Mercè Rodoreda, author of* In Diamond Square

1932, she published her first novel *Soc una dona honrada?* (*Am I an Honourable Woman?*), financed by her husband. She started an affair with a fellow journalist and entered the Bohemian world of the arts in the aftermath of the Primo de Rivera dictatorship. It was in the course of a series of newspaper interviews she conducted with leading Republican figures that she met Andreu Nin, the leader of the POUM and a key figure in the early Civil War, until his murder by Russian agents in 1937. Rodoreda herself fled Cataluña for France the following year with a group of writers. One of them was Joan Prat, with whom she began a lifelong relationship. In exile, she earned a living as a seamstress, writing for her own consumption; the couple then moved to Geneva.

In 1957 the Franco government lifted its prohibition on publishing in Catalan and Rodoreda began to publish her stories in Barcelona. These fictions were vignettes of lower-class life in the city, and many touched the lives of women, as had her 1936 novel *Aloma*, whose central character – who declares that 'love makes me sick' – bears a striking resemblance to her creator in her account of a woman's struggle to live a free life. Her most important work, *In Diamond Square* was published only in 1962, in Barcelona and in

Catalan. Colometa, Pidgey, lived through the span of Barcelona's contemporary history, as did Rodoreda herself – she died in 1983. But unlike Rodoreda, Pidgey lived it close to the ground, experiencing its impact as personal but remote from the causes and forces that were responsible for that history.

Victor Mora, born in 1931, was best known as the writer behind the hugely popular comic book hero Capitán Trueno (Captain Thunder), drawn by Ambros. The Captain first appeared, in full medieval dress, in 1956 and continued his pursuit of justice for the next 40 years. In Franco's Spain, comics were enormously popular – but subject to the same rigid censorship that affected every literary form as well as theatre, film and the press. In his largely autobiographical novel, *Los plátanos de Barcelona* (*The Banana Trees of Barcelona*, 2007), Mora reflects back on his own childhood in post-Civil War Barcelona. He had returned with his mother from France, where his father, a Republican refugee, had died. It is a child's recollection of a city of shortages, scarcity and above all of censorship. While Hitler's *Mein Kampf* was freely and widely on sale, a special permit was required to read Victor Hugo's *Les Miserables*. Mora's sinister pair of villains, Kellner and Gench, the latter certainly ex-SS, had taken refuge in Barcelona after the war and lived by stealing cars. But it is the atmosphere of threat that is captured so well in the novel. At one point an argument erupts between two passengers on a tram:

'Don't shout at me' [says one]. 'Understand? And speak to me in Christian [Castilian Spanish].'

'What do you mean? What do you mean by that remark?' The little man with the umbrella goes pale. He knows very well what the other man means. 'If you don't like it get a taxi.'

'In Spain we speak the imperial language. Is that clearer?' [. . .]

If they had been alone, the little man would have stopped talking. But there, in front of everyone, the offence was too much to bear.

'What do you mean? I don't feel like shutting up [. . .]'

'Be quiet, you bastard. You don't know who you're speaking to.'

Those words, suggesting a mysterious power in the person using them, have come to sound ominous; since the war they have acquired a sinister significance. They sometimes indicate a loudmouth, but almost always come from 'one of the winners' – an ex-prisoner, an ex-soldier – who could demonstrate his membership of the victors with an identity card of some kind. That gave him the right to beat anyone and go unpunished, to arrest someone or have them arrested in the street. A 'winner' who could at any moment cut himself a slice of the victory cake.

This time, the superheroes the kids in the novel are fascinated by will not be able to rescue the victim nor save the world on his behalf. As he grows and looks for work, Lluis goes to the office where Falcón, an accountant, works, only to find he has been arrested. Now he feels the need to understand what this thing is, this communism, that hovers so dangerously in dark corners.

As a writer of comics, Mora would have been subject to the same censorship laws as his fellow artists. Captain Thunder's partner, Sigfrida, was forbidden from wearing a plunging neckline, there would be a minimum number of mentions of God, no swearing and no violence – and this was still imposed in the 1960s. Social issues were touched on only obliquely.

Other writers, in setting their later work in the Franco years, referred to similar incidents and frustrations. Until 1945, local cinema features were preceded by German war documentaries, and Catalan was forbidden until the late 1940s, and then restricted to a small circle of intellectuals concerned with the Catalan classics, among them Tomás Roig, father of the novelist Montserrat Roig. Theatre was heavily censored and restricted largely to light entertainment. The press and radio exclusively used Castilian Spanish.

Sara Moliner's heroine in *The Whispering City* (2016) is hauled off a bus and threatened by fascist thugs for using Catalan in public. And in Juan Marsé's *Ronda de Guinardó* (1984) the nameless inspector, the gnawing pain in his stomach reflecting a deeper unease, furiously enters a draper's shop in whose window he sees displayed together yellow and red textiles and threatens the owner unless the two colours (those of the Catalan flag) are immediately removed.

The first postwar literary prize, the Premio Nadal in 1944, was won by Carmen Laforet with her novel *Nada* (*Nothing*). Hugely popular in Spain, the novel was not translated until four years after the author's death in 2004. Its central character, Andrea, arrives in Barcelona soon after the end of the Civil War to live with her aunt Angustias and her family in their cold and cavernous flat on Carrer Aribau, in the Eixample. As her aunt tells her, the mutual loathing and suspicion within the family echoes the atmosphere in the streets. 'The city is hell,' Angustias says, rife with dangers and menace. Her uncle Juan is brooding and violent, his wife Gloria – abused and ignored – is seduced in her turn by Angustias's brother, Román, a painter of sorts but manipulative and cruel. Andrea's dreams of a new life in the exciting city crash against the suspicion and mutual recrimination in the flat. 'I thought I would be receiving an innocent orphan yearning for affection and instead what I see is rebellious demon,' her aunt tells her before she moves permanently to her favourite convent.

The spare prose style of Laforet's novel is very different from the characteristic tone of the approved literature of her era. Her descriptions of the city and of the family home are reflections of the feelings that pervade its spaces, and her writing maps her responses as she floats alone through the hostile and brutalised environment of the apartment she shares with her dysfunctional family: 'On the blackened walls, you could see the marks of hooked hands, of screams of despair [. . .] Madness smiled from the twisted taps.' When she is left to fend for herself, or when she runs into the Barrio Chino in search of her uncle, what Andrea finds there is a kind of Court of Miracles, poorly lit brothels, threatening old beggars, menace and violence: 'I felt small and squeezed between cosmic forces like the hero in a Greek tragedy.'

These are the sentiments that link her to the existentialist movement then prevailing in France, even though few of the writings of the movement were able to penetrate Francoist censorship. Andrea is, in Sartre's words 'thrown into the world', adrift and alone in an unforgiving environment driven by greed, violence and vengeance. Hence the novel's title.

Despite the harsh living conditions, the rationing and the shortages, a growing number of people moved towards the city through the 1940s. It was a reflection of the hardships faced by the rural population, and to the reputation that Barcelona still enjoyed as a city whose streets were paved with gold. The reality proved to be very different. The absence of freedom, and the generalised repression, coexisted there with the poverty of the majority of its inhabitants. By 1949, 5,000 people were living in caves within the city limits, 60,000 in the shanties in marginal areas like Montjuich, Somorrostro and Carmel, and 150,000 in overcrowded cramped sublets within the city's poorer districts such as the Raval and Barceloneta. These were 'the other Catalans' whose experiences and realities were collected in a series of oral histories and short stories by Francesc Candel. By 1950, the city's population had risen to just below 1.3 million.

In the early 1950s, new geopolitical realities allowed Spain to emerge from its pariah status, even though very little had changed within the country. In the context of the Cold War, the US established a military alliance with Spain which allowed it to build bases on Spanish soil. By the end of the decade, major international companies like Fiat and Pirelli were opening plants in the city. The turning point was the Eucharistic Congress in 1952 which marked Spain's formal acceptance by the Vatican. It was the first time that foreign delegates could attend an international conference in Franco's Spain, even though the visitors were limited to representatives of the Catholic Church, which enjoyed a monopoly position in the regime.

The Congress provides the backdrop to *The Whispering City* by Sara Moliner, a pseudonym for two writers, Rosa Ribas and

Sabine Hoffman, first published in 2013. Its original title, *Don de lenguas* (*The Gift of Tongues*), is a reference to one of the two woman protagonists, Beatriz Noguer, a professor of philology who has been excluded from the university because of her political connections – an experience shared by many intellectuals and academics in those years. The other woman, the younger of the two, is Ana Martí, a journalist at the newspaper *La Vanguardia*, where her father, a well-known journalist in his own right, had worked before his exclusion for political reasons. Ana's role is restricted to the social pages – the role filled these days by *¡Hola!* and its many imitators. But her background and her independence of mind do not fit well with the frivolous self-indulgence of the Franco-supporting wealthy classes of Barcelona. The strange death of one of the socialites she has encountered at these society events provides the opportunity for her to investigate and report what is clearly a murder:

> 'What if it turns out she was killed by someone close to her, a top society person?'
>
> A series of photos of Mariona Sobrerroca in the society pages paraded through Ana's mind, as if she were turning the pages of an album: in evening wear at the Liceo Opera House beside the wives of the city's high-ranking politicians; delivering armfuls of Christmas presents to the children of the Welfare Service, along with several leaders of the Women's Section of the Falange; at a debutante ball; with a group of ladies at a fundraiser for the Red Cross; at dances, concerts, High Mass . . .
>
> 'Well, it would serve as an example of how we are all equal under the law.' The sarcastic tone was still there. 'But I don't think so. It seems to have been a break-in. Whatever it was, we are going to report on it. In an exclusive.'

Her irascible editor accepts that she – a woman and a leftist – will take the case for two reasons. First, his main crime reporter is absent. Second, a case as embarrassing as this on the eve of a Eucharistic

Congress is best left in the hands of someone who will accept and repeat the official explanation, vindicating the police and the justice system in the eyes of the visiting delegates. Ana, of course, is more resolute and persistent than he gives her credit for.

As Ana moves around the city in pursuit of leads and connections, what emerges is a portrait of a city deeply divided by wealth and class and governed by a series of corrupt institutions whose real purpose is to suppress the truth and curtail dissent. Like Mora's protagonist, Ana is threatened by a fascist thug in the street for speaking Catalan. The city she describes is riven with the suspicion, the fear and the paranoia that Laforet described in her novel – the concierges who inform on all the tenants in their buildings, the police whose concern is public order rather than justice, the black marketeers, the servile journalists reporting what is required of them, are all present in the novel – they are the population of 'the whispering city', the aptly chosen title for the novel's English-language edition.

The main police investigator, Isidro Castro, is a Galician – an honourable man in a dishonourable profession, who serves his masters, albeit with his own private resentments. The building on the Via Layetana, where Ana is sent to meet Castro, had a fearsome reputation: oppositionists and dissidents were systematically tortured in its basement cells. What went on behind its doors was widely known, or imagined:

Again Ana felt the anxiety that had seized her when she'd approached the police headquarters. The building was covered in a slick of fear that emanated from its innards, from the basements that were the setting for torture and death. As with so much else, it was something that was known and not talked about. The fear that impregnated the headquarters' walls was nourished by stories told in hushed voices, by unexplained absences whose causes were nonetheless clear, by the cruel echoes of denunciations. Fear penetrated the building's walls and spread into those surrounding it, infecting them. It had reached her as far off as Condal Street, and had gradually tightened around her, crushing her a little more with each step. She had almost forgotten it as she spoke with Castro, but now it was back again, the fear.

Ana's social connections open doors to the parties of the Barcelona elite, whose hypocrisy and corruption prove to be the key to the death of Mariana. In a sense, this is a detective story in a fairly classic mould. But it also offers a well-written portrait of the repressed and frightened Barcelona of the early 1950s. Beatriz's contributions to the investigation are essentially the solving of linguistic puzzles – and the coauthor's professional career in linguistics explains the detailed knowledge Beatriz has of her subject. It is intriguing in its own right, if perhaps a little overworked at times. In the novel and in the time in which it is set, her skills offer a specific benefit. In a society where all speech and text are rigorously controlled, and the truth fabricated by the powerful, it is the subtexts, the hidden references behind words, that hold the secrets. In this case it is precisely those hidden clues that produce the solution and the explanation. And the fact that it is two women who unravel the mystery, against the suspicion and machismo of all their male colleagues, exposes the overpowering apparatus of male dominance that Franco and his sister placed at the centre of their social project.

The Torn Curtain

The year 1959 marked the official end of Spain's isolation, though the military agreements with NATO and the US in 1953 had already given the lie to the independence of Franco's Spain. The arrival of the US Sixth Fleet in 1953, for example, caused a flurry in the city. The US was familiar to most Catalans only from Hollywood cinema, and their image of American sailors derived from films such as *On the Town* (1949) with Gene Kelly or *Anchors*

Aweigh (1952), in which the amiable seamen sing and dance their way through the streets, distributing largesse (especially chocolate and nylons) as they go. The reality was very different. Like most visitors since, they went straight for the Ramblas, turned left into the Raval, where they spent their time in the bars and brothels and behaved, it is reported, like an occupying army.

The internal regime changed little through the 1950s. But the experiment in autarky, in economic self-sufficiency, ended with the Five Year Plan announced in 1959. Foreign investment was invited into this country on the edge of Europe where living standards and therefore wages were far lower. A new wave of immigrants from the rest of Spain travelled towards Barcelona in search of work. There were jobs, but the living standards were low. The new arrivals crowded into the peripheral areas of the city, into the flimsy shacks already there or into the self-built dwellings, with few services, which were all that was available. The corrupt mayor of the city, Josep Maria Porcioles, a faithful servant of Spanish fascism, happily welcomed the new factories, the speculators in construction, and accommodated the city to the growing numbers of cars. The 'Greater Barcelona' he boasted of, however, was a fraud. The city's boundary lines did now include the new barrios, the poor districts like Carmel, Nou Barris and so on, but their inclusion did not signify integration. They remained the territory of the excluded, of the 'other Catalans'.

The end of isolation did not guarantee an instant influx of fresh air. Barcelona did not cease overnight to be a city whose history was denied, its language suppressed, its streets under permanent and aggressive vigilance. Change would come, nevertheless, though it would be neither quick nor natural. The atmosphere of stifling conservatism which writers had described persisted, as did the Franco regime. The economic growth of the subsequent decade would bring benefits to Barcelona, including jobs in the new industrial plants opening there. Yet the influx of people from the poorer regions seeking work created a curious paradox. Encouraged to move, they found the labour market quickly closed and available jobs filled.

The government provided exit visas for Spaniards continuing their search for work in the expanding economies of Europe, in France and Germany in particular. Three million Spaniards would leave in the following decade.

For young people growing up under Franco, the 1950s were a drab and fearful time. For women in particular, the day-to-day repression was unrelenting, beginning in the schools. The writer Montserrat Roig grew up in the Eixample, a district of comfortable middle- and upper-middle-class families. Her family was progressive and critical of the prevailing order, in contrast to the oppressive atmosphere that Andrea, Carmen Laforet's protagonist in *Nada*, found when she lived there, just as Roig did at her convent school, as exaplined in Betsabé García's biography of Roig, *Amb uns altres ulls Ed Roca* (2016): 'I was educated into victimhood, resignation and the fear of being ourselves. And women who have been intellectually castrated cannot move beyond mental self-mutilation.'

This was clearly not the case for Roig, however. Despite the fact that her parents – her father a Catalan intellectual, her mother a writer – said very little about the war, they did not interfere in the radical direction their daughter's life was taking. By the mid-1960s there was some cautious development of Catalan culture. Under the umbrella of the art school, a new theatre school, the Escuela Nacional Dramática Adriá Gual (ENDAG), began to offer plays in Catalan in the Brechtian manner, under its co-founders Ricardo Salvat and Maria Aurelia Capmany. They resolved to 'have done with the embarrassing folkloric theatre to which Catalan drama had been reduced'. An early example of their work was a play by the outstanding poet and public opponent of the Franco regime, Salvador Espriu, *La primera historia de Esther* (*Esther's First Story*) first published in 1948 and presented at ENDAG in 1982. Its cast included the young Montserrat Roig, who very soon began to write stories and essays focusing on the situation of women in Franco's Spain.

Roig was involved in the protest occupation of the Capuchin monastery at Sarrià in Barcelona in 1966, but escaped the beatings meted out to other demonstrators because the police did not con-sider it possible that women would be involved in public protests. International condemnation followed, and six major artists contrib-uted works to an auction in Paris to pay the huge fines imposed on the organisers.

Roig was a regular interviewer for the first newspaper to be published in Catalan since the war, *Tele/Xpres*. Her interviews, at first in print and later on television, became a cast list of the new Catalan (and Spanish) culture. They were later published in two separate volumes. Her questioning is forthright and insistent but, taken together, her conversations are the soundtrack of change. The sexual revolution, the feminism she and others brought back from France and the activism she expressed through her sometimes uneasy relationship with the PSUC (the Catalan Communist Party) gave her a key role in the process of change. Equally important was her research into the experience of Catalans in Nazi camps, an early contribution to her generation's confrontation of the past. It emerged that 6,000 Catalans had died in Mauthausen alone, and that many others had experienced the horrors of other concentration and extermination camps.

Roig's 1977 novel, *Els temps de cereres* (*Cherry Time*), forms part of a trilogy about three generations of bourgeois women living out their lives in the Eixample. Its central character, Natalia Miralpeix, like her creator, had participated in the student rebellions of 1962. A photographer (modelled on Roig's lifelong friend and collaborator Pilar Almeyrich), she left Barcelona after the demonstrations and returned only at the end of 1974. Her return is clearly a journey of self-discovery, or is intended as such, and a search for explanations. She returns to a family that enclosed itself in the silent inner places of the domestic space, as if closing the doors and windows not only on the street but on the past:

> They had to leave behind what had brought them so much misfortune. They had to change their way of thinking, begin to

speak in a different way, dress the way they wanted them to, shut themselves in the house, sleep, submerge themselves in a long, deep sleep, and not go out into the street, because the street belonged to them.

She senses a kind of shame mixed with fear – 'they' is the outside world, the society dominated by Spanish fascism. In 1963 the trial of Julian Grimau, a leading communist poet who was executed after a summary military court sentenced him to death, was a defiant display of strength by the regime in the aftermath of student risings in the city. There were international protests, but the regime was indifferent to them. Twelve years later, in 1974, as Natalia returned, one of the last victims of the dictatorship's garrote, Salvador Puig Antich, was executed. Her Barcelona has changed. It was now the city of Porcioles, who was mayor from 1957 to 1973. Notoriously corrupt, his vision of the city was all fast cars and wide avenues, consumer culture and a self-conscious and ostentatious modernity which proclaimed itself the face of the future, but without reference to the past. Each of the novel's narrative voices responds evasively to the changes. Her brother Luis takes his lead from James Dean, her sister-in-law accumulates consumer goods and eats excessive quantities of cake. Her widowed father buys gifts for his beloved departed wife to assuage his grief. What in the early 1960s had been a joyful and affirmative eruption into the streets, an occupation of public space, had now become a purposeful flight past shop windows in what Roig describes as 'una ciudad desventrada', a city with its guts torn out. As she wanders the city streets, Natalia remembers that they were once the site of all that was forbidden, dangerous, transgressive. Now they are merely another interior, filled with what Walter Benjamin called the 'phantasmagoria' of modern life.

A Generation Rediscovers Its Past

The new generation, in some sense, had to reinvent their culture. The previous generation of writers and artists had either died or gone into exile, and those that remained were denied the Catalan language and were subject to an intense and generalised censorship, quite apart from the networks of informers placed in the concierge's flat in every apartment block. Catalan culture, for nearly two decades, developed outside the country, in Europe or in Latin America, particularly in Mexico. But as the writer Manuel Vázquez Montalbán put it in his *Barcelonas*, 'Years after the deluge, the young students of the forties were in a position to recall their own adolescence; they offered a depressing picture of what remained after the disaster, and the few islands of culture to which they could turn to research and reconstruct, at least at the level of imagination, their lost Atlantis.'

Some of the exiles had begun to return in the 1950s but continued to live in a kind of internal exile, unrecognised, invisible and unemployed – like the poet Carles Ribas who was never allowed to return to his job at the university. Others, equally marginalised, maintained a clandestine existence in private readings and gatherings. Vázquez Montalbán quotes the poet Pere Quart's response to all those who had written odes to Barcelona across the years:

> Barcelona, consider this.
> Do not sing. Look into your heart, beating now so hard that it
>   could burst.
> Don't stop. Cry a little every day.
> When the earth starts to turn again, keep your eyes closed.
> One step at a time.
> Don't be distracted by the leaves carried off by the wind,
> Or by the new wings that are foretold.
> Work silently. Distrust history.
> Dream it and remake it.

Keep your eye on the sea, on the mountains.
Think of the child you are carrying within.

The secret poetry readings in bookshops and private flats were signs of an emerging generation deprived of its culture and its language and enraged by the suffocating atmosphere in their society. There had been protest movements in the 1950s; the 1951 tram boycott was one (described in Moliner's *The Whispering City*), and the protests after the invasion of Hungary in 1956, another. An underground workers' movement was also reawakening by the end of the decade. The new generation of writers and poets had few familiar precedents but the returning exiles brought back their memories of the cultural flowering under the Republic, and the Catalan they had continued to use in Mexico or France. For those writers, their audience restricted to a small circle in a distant Mexico, this was a double exile, not mitigated, at least at first, on their return to a city where Catalan was still largely (but no longer entirely) banned outside the private sphere.

It fell to those who remained to give new impetus to the process of change that the new contacts with Europe, for all their limitations, would offer. It was not easy to travel out of Spain and then return. The flow of returning exiles did slowly increase, but not because there was any marked liberalisation of the regime. The state remained deeply hostile to all things Catalan – and to all things democratic.

In the early 1960s currents of renovation in the Catholic Church symbolised by Pope John XXIII and his liberal encyclicals had a major influence. The Catalan Church was as divided as the society itself; some of its priests were committed social reformers – and there was discontent among the younger Catalan clergy about the role that the Catholic hierarchy had played in the suppression of Catalan cultural rights. The monastery at Montserrat, whose services were held in Catalan, became a key symbol of the battle for language rights. More radical still were the worker priests, the movement that began in France and which spilled across the border into Spain as priests in overalls joined those working and living in the city.

In 1963, a young singer-songwriter, Raimón, won the Mediterranean Song Competition with a song in Catalan 'S'en va anar' ('We're on Our Way'), though his 'Al vent' ('To the Wind') had already become hugely popular (and remains so). Raimón was slightly younger than Els Setze Juges (Sixteen Judges), the group founded in 1961 to promote the Cançó Nova (New Song), the movement to promote Catalan music, but he became one of its leading members. The regime had largely ignored the Cançó until Raimón's success alerted them to the impact it was already having in the ignored undergrowth of Catalan culture. Their music was inspired by the French chanson of Brassens, Moustaki and Brel rather than the protest music of Britain and the US, and like the French singers' work, it was in many senses a very literary movement.

The texts of the songs of Luis Llach, Joan Manuel Serrat, Maria del Mar Bonet and Raimón were often settings of the words of forbidden poets – Salvador Espriu, Pere Quart, Salvat-Papasseit – writing in Catalan. By the end of the decade, and despite a hardening of censorship, their songs remained both the expression and the symbol of a resurgent Catalan national consciousness. To sing Raimón's 'Al vent', Luis Llach's 'Cançó dels mans' ('Song of the Hands') or Serrat's setting of Antonio Machado's poem 'Caminante' – 'Caminante no hay camino, / Se hace camino al andar' (Traveller, there is no road, / You make it as you go) – was in itself an act of resistance. The Institute of Catalan Studies, cautiously reopened with a brief to limit itself to the Catalan classics, was closed again in 1967. It was a futile attempt to stem a gathering tide.

 8

LOOKING DOWN FROM
THE HILLS

In December 1977, Anthony Burgess and his wife boarded the luxurious Talgo express in Geneva, en route to Barcelona, 'this jewel of Catalonia', as he described it in his 'Homage to Barcelona', published in the *New York Times*:

Our Andalusian taxi driver – he says e'pañole' instead of españoles and he had come to Cataluña because that is where Spaniards who want to work always come [. . .] He takes us up to Tibidabo, high up on the Sierra of Collserola from which you can look down on the entire city and the Mediterranean beyond (another way up would have been by funicular from the Columbus statue). The name Tibidabo comes from Christ's promise to Peter according to the Vulgate 'Tibi dabo clavia regni caelorum' – To Thee I will give the keys of the kingdom of heaven. To justify the religious intitulation of a splendiferous park of secular attractions – a ferris wheel, museums, observatory, bars – there is a great Templo Expiatorio de España (suggesting there is always guilt beneath gaiety) topped by a Christ with his arms spread winglike over the sea and the city.

If Tibidabo is a wonder, Montjuich is a marvel. I take it the Catalan name means Mountjoy, that is, Paradise, and like heaven it has no truck with space or time. A complete artificial city called the Pueblo Español was built for the Exposición Internacional of 1929. In it you can literally walk through the whole of Spain, if by Spain you mean not dusty distances on donkeyback but the cultures, cuisines and architecture of all the Spanish provinces. There too is the Museo de Arte de Cataluña (the Museum of Catalan Art), which shows very firmly that Catalonian painting and sculpture go back a long way, are autonomous, indigenous, a straight line from the Byzantine-like Christographs to Miro and Picasso [. . .] Catalan pride in an ancient and continuous culture has, of course, profound political consequences.

Last Tram to Tibidabo

The best way to travel to Tibidabo is on the old tram, the only one that has survived, that puffs and groans its way up the steep Avenida Tibidabo. From there a funicular takes you up the hill to the funfair or the church, built in the style of Paris's Sacré Coeur, whichever is your preference. The Avenida Tibidabo is an avenue of grand mansions spaced widely apart. Some are still occupied by a single family, but most are now schools, or convents, institutions or businesses.

In Ruiz Zafón's *Shadow of the Wind* the eerie mansion at number 32 plays a central role in the story.

The storm's icy blast blurred the ghostly outline of mansions, and large, rambling houses veiled in the mist. Among them rose the dark and solitary tower of the Aldaya mansion, anchored among the swaying trees [. . .] The small door encased within the gates swung in the wind. Beyond it, a path wound its way up to the house [. . .] Through the undergrowth I could make out the pedestals of statues that had been knocked down. As I neared the mansion, I noticed that one of the statues, the figure of an avenging angel, had been dumped into the fountain that was the centerpiece of the garden.

The scene is pure Gothic horror, though the majority of the houses, built at the turn of the century, would be more Modernista in style than Gothic. It may be that the house described here was one of two on the avenue designed by Gaudí's contemporary Puig i Cadafalch, whose work always includes Gothic as well as Modernista elements. The nineteenth-century novelist Vicente Blasco Ibáñez explains it this way in his *Mare nostrum* (1918):

> The commercial bourgeoisie have covered the area with architectural decorations worthy of their fantasies. Shopkeepers and factory owners wanted a house for pleasure, traditionally called 'torres', to relax in on Sundays but also to display their property. There were houses in the Gothic, Arab, Greek and Persian manner. The more patriotic among them placed their faith in the inspirations of a group of architects who had invented a Catalan art [. . .] Ferragut walked along the empty street, lined by two rows of recently planted trees which were just beginning to produce their early buds. He looked at the façades of the 'torres', made with blocks of cement imitating the stone of ancient fortresses, and covered by tiles representing dream-like landscapes, curious flowers and nymphs with a blue haze.

Montjuich, on the other hand, looks down directly onto the port and the city below. It was a military emplacement from the eighteenth century onwards, its cannons directed towards the streets below like its reflection on the other side of the city, the Ciutadella. Until the early twentieth century it was occupied only by the fort and the stone quarries that supplied the stone for Santa María del Mar and other buildings in the Gothic Quarter. It was the 1929 Exposition that incorporated the hill into the city. Burgess is wrong to interpret its name as referring to paradise; it means the Hill of the Jews, a reference to the Jewish cemetery that occupied part of the hillside. The home of the Museum of Catalan Art, the Pueblo Español and the Teatre Grec were, as we have seen, built for the

1929 Exposition, as was the Modernist pavilion designed by Mies van der Rohe – the present building is a replica rebuilt in 1986. It was transformed again for the 1992 Olympics.

Home to the wonderful Miró Foundation, which you can reach by funicular railway or by the cable car from the port, Montjuich's history and its role in the city is represented by a less obvious place for visitors, the Fossar de las Pedreres, the quarries which are now a cemetery. Here are stone monuments commemorating Lluis Companys, the president of the Catalan Republic shot in the fortress in 1940, Francesc Ferrer, the libertarian teacher executed after the Semana Trágica of 1909 as a reprisal for the disturbances. The castle may look strange and magical, but it was a prison and a barracks for most of its life, and many atrocities were committed there.

It is from the vantage point of Montjuich that Alvaro, the narrator of Juan Goytisolo's important novel *Marks of Identity* (1966) looks down on the city through a telescope in the final, breathless stream of consciousness with which the novel ends:

The city you were looking at, was it yours

the flock of tourists had disappeared behind the guide and following the instructions written to the right and left of the telescope you put another coin in the slot and pushed the button all the way down

you examined in turn [. . .]

in this same environment of burned earth remote sky impossible birds obsessive light

during the reign of the Twenty-Five Years of Peace recognised and celebrated by all right-thinking people in the world

armed men had beaten defenseless fellow countrymen with whips lashes rifles had vent their fury on them with butts ropes boots guns [. . .]

Although it was published in Mexico in 1966, it would be another ten years before the novel was distributed and published in Spain (by

Seix Barral). It is ahead of its time both in its form and in its content. Its combination of multiple texts and styles, and its range of narrative voices, were characteristic of the contemporary New Latin American novel of Gabriel García Márquez and Mario Vargas Llosa, who had adopted Barcelona as a second home. By this time Barcelona was beginning to assert itself as a centre for the publication of literature in Castilian Spanish, with its new publishing houses, including Seix Barral, Tusquets and 62 Ediciones. But in Spain in the mid-1960s the form was still unusual (what is often regarded as the first Castilian experimental novel, *Tiempo de silencio* (*A Time of Silence*) by the Madrid-based writer Luis Martín-Santos, was published in 1962).

The three Goytisolo brothers came from a progressive lower-middle-class family living in central Barcelona – an early experience Juan would return to in his 1999 autobiography *Coto vedado* (*Forbidden Territory*). But Alvaro Mendiola, the protagonist of his *Marks of Identity*, comes from a very different background. Alvaro is from a landowning *indiano* family who made their money in the plantation economy of Cuba and the slave trade that supplied it. Alvaro leaves Barcelona in the early 1950s for France and becomes a photographer for the France Presse agency. Born in 1931, Alvaro spends most of the period of the Civil War in the south of France, where his family have taken refuge in anticipation of the victory of Catholic and conservative Spain and the defeat of the Republic. His father is killed on the first day of the war, however, outside the village of Yeste. The villagers there had lost their lands (and their livelihood) when they disappeared with the construction of a dam in 1934. In fact, the construction was never completed, nor did they receive the promised compensation from the governments of the Republic. Their expectation was that the victory of the Popular Front in February 1936 would bring them justice. When it did not, they occupied lands that belonged to the Mendiolas, which they considered communal property. They refused to leave and were gunned down by the Civil Guard. Days later, Alvaro's father was executed by local anarchist militias.

In 1963, Alvaro returns to Barcelona to make a documentary that will allow him to discover his own identity, his own allegiances – and his own responsibilities. He was part of the first generation of students to protest publicly against Franco – in 1951, with the tram boycott (which figures in the novel). Unlike his friends at the time, he did not stay, but left instead for Paris, where he would remain for ten years. He was among many Spaniards in exile – often in Madame Berger's café – but their reasons for being there varied widely.

> Alvaro had observed that the members of each historical layer maintained only a superficial connection with groups before or after them, obeying an implicit but scrupulously respected set of rules. The first group – to which Alvaro belonged – were political or intellectual emigrés who for the most part crossed the Pyrenees, with or without a passport, after a longer or shorter spell in jail [. . .] because of their participation in student movements or other protests.

But these did not include people like Alvaro, who essentially left for family reasons. The second group included those who had crossed the border secretly in order to join the Maquis between 1944 and 1950; a third represented those who had left Spain at the end of the Civil War and had found themselves interned and forced to work in labour camps or factories but miraculously escaped death in Auschwitz. (Alan Resnais's moving 1969 film *La guerre est finie* (*The War is Over*) is set among the exiles.) Recovering in Paris after a heart attack, Alvaro returns to seek out his past and thus his own identity. But the Spain he finds is no longer the society the exiles dreamed of returning to. The impact of the fascist system that was imposed on the country after the Civil War has been to create a society dominated by fear. Police reports on the surveillance of Alvaro's friends appear throughout the novel; their function in the text is not immediately obvious, until this:

The reign of Twenty Five Years of Peace was only the visible product of the underground activity over generations dedicated to the noble and joyful mission of maintaining through hell and high water the rigid and unmoving principles, the necessary respect for the law, the swift and blind obedience to the mysterious norms that govern a society divided into categories and social classes [. . .] As a result of this long and valuable experience the people began to apply these cathartic rules to itself, and in that false summer of 1963 [Alvaro's] country had become a somnolent nation of thirty or so million police without uniforms.

Alvaro's Barcelona was a city that, even then, was becoming dominated by tourism, to which it owed, in good part, its economic rebirth. When he returns to Yeste, where his father had been killed, it brings home to him how completely the past has been buried. Filming his documentary, which is confiscated by the police, he arrives when the town is celebrating the running of the bulls – the ceremony for which San Fermin is famous – and has forgotten the massacre of its own just a few years before. Looking down on Barcelona through the telescope he sees a city which is also in danger of forgetting.

the Puerta de la Paz La Barceloneta the thick smoke from the
   factories
but no
that is not their victory
and if a fate that is harsh for you as it was for the others takes you
   away
without your wishing
before you see the life of your country and its men restored
leave evidence at least of this time do not forget what happened
   there do not be silent
the chaotic geometry of the city the three chimneys of La
   Canadiense belfries and spires of churches gardens [. . .]

Perhaps someone will understand later
What order you tried to resist and what your crime was
INTRODUZCA LA MONEDA
INSERT COIN

The Hidden Heights

The view of the city from the wealthier districts around Tibidabo
and Sarrià was very different from the panorama seen from
Gaudí's Parc Guell. The park was originally planned as an
exclusive gated housing estate, with the Catalan 'parc' replaced
by an English 'park'. But the houses did not sell, and the park –
with its extraordinary tile-coated animals and its sinuous concrete
structures – became a popular leisure space for Barcelona's citizens;
today it is a vastly overcrowded magnet for tourists limited to half-
hour time slots. Few visitors leave the park from its rear entrance.
If they did, it would take them to a very different world – Monte
Carmel and Guinardó.

As Anthony Burgess points out, Barcelona has been an objective
for those seeking work from the poorer regions of Spain for recent
generations. His Andalucian taxi driver was one. In the 1940s,
when conditions in the countryside were particularly harsh, the
rhythm of migration increased and continued into the 1950s. These
new Barcelonans moved into the poorer districts. The Raval, which
had traditionally offered refuge to the poor, had reached bursting
point, and the slab-like tower blocks of Monte Carmel offered
some kind of shelter, though facilities and services were minimal.
On Montjuich a shanty town, Can Tunis, spread across the hill
beneath the fortress. And Barceloneta, long since spilling beyond its
geometric streets, took in other poor workers.

Between 1945 and 1970 1.5 million new residents arrived
in the city, to receive poor living conditions and low wages. In
Barceloneta, Somorrostro became emblematic of the new slums –

it was significant that Carmen Amaya, one of the flamenco stars of the era, was born and raised there, among Andalucian migrants. These new immigrants were Castilian Spanish speakers.

In the poorer districts of Barcelona, and in the new workplaces, strikes and protests were evidence of a new trade unionism, and a new militancy – repressed with none of the delicacy shown, at least occasionally, to middle-class demonstrators. Many of this new generation of workers lived in the poor barrios scattered along the hills above the city, many of the houses self-built, and most with minimal services. They were *Les altres Catalans* (*The Other Catalans*) a phrase coined by the writer who became their chronicler, Francesc Candel. His 1965 work written under that title, in both Catalan and Castilian, is at once oral history, sociological analysis of these poor hillside communities, and short stories which gather the experiences and the voices of the marginalised population. He was extraordinarily prolific in his writings, but his most significant work was published in the late 1950s. *Donde la ciudad cambia su nombre* (*Where the City Changes its Name*, 1957) and *Han matado a un hombre, han roto un paisaje* (*A Man Has Been Killed, a Landscape Has Been Destroyed*, 1959) are both novels rooted in the reality of the poor communities where Candel grew up. They were published in paperback at low prices and with dramatic realist covers; they have a ring of immediacy and authenticity to which his readers obviously responded, since for many of them it was their own lives that were depicted. Candel's later work, more consciously political, tended to be sociological and perhaps more distanced from the direct experience of his subjects. Both were censored by the Franco regime, as was most of his work; they were later republished in full.

Candel's work was, implicitly, a response to an allegation from some sections of Catalan society that these immigrant workers did not belong in the city, since many had travelled from Murcia and Andalucia in search of work. In reply, Candel quotes a teacher who asked how many of his students were Catalan. Just three or four raised their hands. But a dozen more non-Catalans then raised their hands to claim that they too were Catalans. In the context of the suppression of the language by Franco, the anxiety about its survival is understandable. But what Candel shows, in fact, is that the children of these workers considered themselves to be Catalans too. The important division in the city, for Candel, was not between Catalan and non-Catalan speakers, but between the marginal districts, the *suburbios*, and the wealthy *zonas*, home to Barcelona's rich – a divide growing constantly wider.

Juan Marsé was a leading figure among the writers emerging in Barcelona from the 1960s onwards. A writer from a young age, his works were set largely in the working-class areas surrounding the city, particularly Carmel and Guinardó. He writes entirely in Castilian, perhaps to reflect the people he writes about. Like Goytisolo and others, his first novel was published in Mexico, and it would take a further ten years and the death of Franco before it was possible for him to be read in his native city. Two novels especially won him a significant reading public. *Ultimas tardes con Teresa* (*Last Evenings with Teresa*) was published in 1966. Teresa is a girl from a wealthy suburb; Pijoaparte lives in Carmelo, in the Horta-Guinardó area. His family are immigrants from Murcia, like many of the inhabitants of the slum districts that developed in the mountains behind the city. He regularly gatecrashes parties, and on this occasion manages to join one in a big house in a middle-class district, where he meets and seduces Maruja, thinking she is one of the guests. She is in fact a maid to Teresa's family, though Pijoaparte will not discover that until much later. His ambitions, however, are to conquer a rich girl and perhaps to find a route out of the poor districts on the hill, away from the shabby bar where he drinks. Teresa is part of a generation of university students becoming radicalised with the relative thaw in the social atmosphere of Barcelona in the 1960s. She goes on demonstrations, has been part of a theatre group taking Brecht to the shop floor and expresses her desire for 'a companionship based on solidarity, without class barriers'. Pijoaparte takes her expressions of sympathy and solidarity with the working class seriously and claims to belong to a trade union in a factory and feigns interest in her ideas: '"This is a time of transition, don't you think? I'm talking about moral values, which are in decline." The university student then began to develop her theory about the current crisis of love.'

Part of his interest in Teresa, of course, is sexual. But beyond that is the escape from the constraints of his class. The irony is palpable, since Teresa herself is seduced largely by his social background. But when he takes her to the local dance in Carmelo she is shocked, all the more so when his claim to be a worker militant is exposed. The poor maid, who has simply been used by both Teresa and Pijo, dies. In the poignant ending and despite all the progressive rhetoric, the barriers between the two young lovers prove insuperable. In Marsé's beautifully written and carefully crafted novels, these themes recur, as does their setting.

Most of Juan Marsé's works are set in the area of the Guinardó, where he was brought up, the area between Gracia and what, until the 1950s, was the largely agricultural area of Horta. The expansion of Barcelona from the early 1950s onwards brought a speculative construction boom, building basic cheap housing for immigrant workers. Marsé's description of the area is vivid, and unblinking in its description of the poverty and alienation of its marginal populations. Marsé returns to the area in his extremely successful and compelling novel *Si te dicen que cai* (*If They Tell You that I Fell*, 1973). As his translator Nick Caistor has underlined, Marsé is harsh in his description of the material world of Monte Carmelo, but his characters – the people of the poor barrios – have wit and insight and, above all, a rich imaginative universe. The youngsters in the post-Civil War city of the 1940s suffer privations of every kind, and the endless persecution of police and priests who impose the disciplines of a fascist society. They have no alternative references, other than a vague and still immediate family history, a collective memory of the city as changed, albeit briefly, during the Civil War. But it is not a sentimental recollection.

The reality of their lives in the barrio is reflected in *If They Tell You* in the language of the community. In some ways his protagonists in the novel speak in a choral voice; at times one speaker elides into another. But their experience is common. Here the boys build a 'refuge' in the rubble of an old church and recreate scenes from the films they have seen in the local cinema (when they have managed to get in without paying). With the distorted innocence of kids living in the brutal conditions of the hilltop slums, they seize on the violence and twisted sexuality of what they have seen – the torture of women, the threat of rape and imprisonment – exacerbated with the stories on the street leaked from prison and the torture centre at Barcelona's Via Layetana.

The central character lives in a rag-and-bone shop. But from a very young age she is used as a prostitute, pandering to the perversions of a new culture whose high moral values are contradicted every day in their reality. The women of this universe are prostituted in many ways. So many of them have lost husbands and companions to the war or they are locked up in prison. And those who do return, like the group of anarchists around Palau and Luis Lage, are determined to develop an armed urban guerrilla group funded by bank robberies and theft. One by one they are caught and killed. In a society where everything is conducted in whispers and fuelled by rumour, it is hard to escape the ubiquitous armed police, though Palau and Luis do stay free for the next 20 years. Meeting then in their favourite bar, the Alaska, they repeat the mantra of earlier times – 'It will never last.' Other voices repeat the futile hope:

We thought yes. We said no. We thought this won't last, we'll hold out. The sirens won't sound any more. The national anthem will accompany the raising of the communion cup. There are no more entries into hiding places vomiting into the night the screams of mothers, they will not come back to kill children from the sky. From now on, boys, the danger will be everywhere and nowhere, the threat will be invisible and constant [. . .] The speaker is a boy from Carmelo. There's not much in his stories that is true, until time changes that, because this boy tells stories based not only on the bloody events of the past but also on things to come. He talks about bombs skulking in the grass that will explode years later, of venomous scorpions that will survive in the ruins, of tattoos and scars on the memory that can never be removed. In a tiny attic barely lit by a single candle, he says, sitting in a rocking chair making paper birds out of old magazines, day and night, thinking of a pretty girl wearing rubber boots, of the brave comrades loyal to the death.

Marsé's is not the world of the Raval, with its perverted glamour and its revolutionary past. As Michael Eaude puts it in his *Barcelona*, there is no smell of gunpowder here. Marsé's Barcelona of the 1940s is in the district that grew up on the hills behind Gracia, where kids struggle to survive. The games the boys play in the bomb-sites re-enact the defeat the anarchists talk over endlessly in the local bars: 'today as it did yesterday and will do tomorrow, everything in the barrio stays the same. It has all been over for years, and today it is just as over.'

Yet it did end, as dictatorships so often do. The hopes for which the Civil War was fought also fade into memory, and they are left, looking into an uncertain future. 'Men of iron, forged in so many battles, now dreaming like children', in the closing words of *If They Tell You that I Fell*.

The Pact of Forgetting

The instant transformation did not happen, and the forgotten past remained forgotten as the politicians of the new era wanted it, perhaps to avoid reliving the old conflicts over and over again (like the ageing anarchists) or perhaps to avoid facing the evasions and unexplored responsibilities that looking into the past would have demanded. That at least was the consensus among those who took over power after 1975 when they agreed to the Pacto del Olvido, the Pact of Forgetting.

Yet there were some initial significant changes. Perhaps most importantly, the 'linguistic normalisation', officially approved in 1980, and the adoption of Catalan as the official language of Cataluña and of its political and commercial life. The Catalan-language television channel, TV3, began in the early 1980s, and a vibrant publishing industry turned its attention to Catalan-language publication in the same period. The moral atmosphere changed dramatically, as the underground culture emerged into the public space and sexual freedom became the norm. Yet the availability of pornography and the sexualised cinema typified by the work of Bigas Luna did not of themselves guarantee a genuine transformation of the lives of women in Spain. That remained to be fought for. And there was a double-edged consequence of the opening up of the Raval as the Ramblas became, by the mid-1980s, the haunt of drug traffickers and users.

The process of uncovering the past had begun earlier. Pere Calders, for example, lived in exile in Mexico before returning to Barcelona in 1962. Before the Civil War he had won a reputation as a cartoonist and short-story writer, and he continued to write – in Catalan – in exile. One volume he published there in the mid-1950s – *Cróniques de la verita oculta* (*Chronicles of a hidden truth*) (1955) – could well serve as a general title for his writings. The tales are brief narratives, often with an unreliable narrator, that move between realism and a magical realm which progressively intrudes on the otherwise everyday world.

The collection was published in English as *The Virgin of the Railway and Other Stories* (1991). In 'A Natural History', the narrator's modern apartment is gradually transformed into a jungle with a tiger living in his kitchen. When he complains to the concierge in his block of flats, the concierge shrugs his shoulders and recommends leaving water – as if this metamorphosis were wholly unremarkable. In 'An American Curio', a strange visitor brings a gun and then dies in his unwilling host's sitting room. Unclear who his visitor is or where he has come from, the narrator simply hangs the cadaver in his wardrobe and goes on holiday. Calders became well known at a late age when the theatre company Dagoll Dagom adapted some of his stories for a highly successful show, *Antaviana*, based on a story by Calders in which a schoolboy invents a magical world to which he can escape from the boredom of the classroom.

Formed in 1974, Dagoll Dagom's spectacular musical productions moved between realism and a profound sense of the magical. Their work, entirely in Catalan, has revived or rediscovered Catalan literature and poetry, from Calders to the reworking of a text by the major popular dramatist of the late nineteenth century, Angel Guimera. Dagoll Dagom's version of Guimera's *Mar i cel* (*Sea and Sky*), set on a pirate ship, explores racism and intolerance through a love story between a North African corsair and a Spanish woman. It was chosen for revival for the group's fortieth anniversary in 2014.

The work of Manuel del Pedrolo, who was born in 1918, was extremely popular during the 1960s and 1970s. A polemical essayist, novelist and short-story writer, he wrote entirely in Catalan – a reflection of his unwavering commitment to Catalan independence. That was one reason why he was mostly unpublished until the end of the Franco regime. Yet he was enormously prolific throughout his life. He was always an experimenter, moving in and out of different literary genres, from the detective story to science fiction. The clue to his work is in his contributions to theatre, and specifically as a pioneer of the theatre of the absurd in Spain. Pedrolo's narrative skill, and the enormous breadth of his writing, was acknowledged early, even though he would have to wait for publication until after the dictatorship. His early writing was more explicitly political, but his most successful work (with over 40 editions) was his *Mecanoscrit del secon origen* (*Typescript of the Second Origin*, 1975), a dystopian science-fiction novel especially popular with the young, possibly because of its protagonists. Alba (who is 12) and Didac (a boy of six) survive an alien holocaust because they are both underwater when it happens. Despite the death and destruction that surround them they set out to explore their devastated Cataluña and then travel further, remaking the world in a spirit of friendship and later love. The typescript, a found document, is written after Didac's death by an adult Alba – her name, meaning dawn, suggesting that a new civilisation will emerge with their child.

The novel has not been translated. But *Trajecte final* (*Final Trajectory*, 1974) has been rendered into English. It is a collection of rather strange stories, less narratives than symbolic metaphors stripped down to their basic elements, but certain themes that are repeated throughout Pedrolo's work are treated there. The oppression of women, their reduction to their sexual function, is a constant in his writing. Thus in the story 'Cadàvers' a burglar enters a Paris flat to find three dead women, apparently prostitutes, on the floor. Surprised that there are no reports of their murder, he returns to the flat to find another woman there, Olga, a receptionist. They later sleep together and it emerges that she, like the three victims, is a robot. In several other stories, while the setting is minimally described, it is clear that we are in an alienated modern universe of mysterious multinationals and office blocks where people are 'disappeared' or reproduced in a series of parallel universes, and that the 'Total Census' of another story is a global register which allows earth's inhabitants to be cloned. In a sense the stories are all metaphors, stagings of philosophical problems which absorbed Pedrolo, as a reader and translator of French literature.

It was in theatre that the wider avant-garde movements had their first impact, in part because they were able to sidestep the mechanisms of censorship. The importance of Marcel Marceau and Jacques LeCoq, the key figures in the growth of mime in theatre, enabled the first groups of the new independent theatre movement in Barcelona – Els Joglars (the Troubadours) formed in 1966, Els

Comediants (the Comic Actors) in 1970 and Dagoll Dagom in 1974 – to develop a new and revolutionary form of theatre. The use of mime, music and circus skills were not easily censored, and the collective practices of the theatre companies enabled them to operate at first on a smaller budgets than equivalent theatre companies.

Further, they were developing a theatre in public spaces, where their extravagant sets, papier mâché giant heads, clowns and comedians connected to popular traditions outside conventional theatre. They were, nonetheless, remorseless critics of the Franco regime, though it is ironic that the first time the iconic leader of Els Joglars, Alberto Boadella, was arrested and forced into exile was in 1977, two years after Franco's death, in response to a play about the torture and execution of Puig Antich and his fellow detainee, Heinz Creeh. In later decades these three great companies, together with La Fura dels Baus and others, would dominate the circuit of international festivals with their large-scale spectacles – though it might be said sometimes at the expense of their engagement with their own reality.

Barcelona was emerging from nearly four decades of Franco's neo-fascist dictatorship. The occupation of Montserrat in 1970 marked the beginning of a major change. The Assemblea de Catalunya that emerged from the event, and which was formally established in 1972, represented a broad consensus in favour of Catalan autonomy. The demand for change was growing in strength in many sectors. The Comisiones Obreras (CCOO – Workers' Commissions) launched in 1966 from a church in the Sants district had grown, as had the level of trade union activity, as the official 'vertical' trade unions increasingly became empty shells. The urban development fostered by Porcioles had benefited speculators, hotel enterprises and tourism, but urban housing – or rather its absence – remained a pressing problem and gave rise to new forms of residents' associations fighting for services and improvement to their conditions. They arose at the grassroots, because there was no form of authentic representation to which they could turn in the official institutions, still governed as they were by the appointees of Franco's authoritarian system.

At another level, a new generation of architects watched with horror as historic Barcelona was threatened with demolition. In 1974 G. Gill's *Barcelona* presented what was in effect a manifesto to save the city from the developers. The Barcelona that attracts so many visitors today to its Modernista buildings, for example, owes much to those who mobilised at that time in defence of its patrimony. And there were other signs of imminent change. Manuel Vázquez Montalbán notes that the previously hidden drag culture of the Chinese Quarter was now increasingly surfacing – a certain sign, in his view, of the moral transformations already under way.

In *Temps de cereres*, Montserrat Roig's returning exile, Natalia, was struck by how grey the city was in 1974. Two years later, after waiting so long, the city received the news of Franco's death in curious silence. The functionaries and beneficiaries of his regime held their breath. The protests and demonstrations of the preceding years suggested that the city would explode after so many years of suppression. Instead, there was a very different sort of explosion – a hedonistic riot. The newspaper kiosks on the Ramblas had been selling the works of Marx and Engels for some time. Now the *destape* – the sudden explosion as the lid was removed from the pressure cooker – produced a proliferation of pornography and a kind of public pleasure-seeking. Barcelona became a sexually liberated area. Or at least so it appeared.

It seemed that, despite its reputation, Barcelona was no more liberated than other major cities where gay culture had become familiar and mainstream. And transvestism and transsexual prostitution are not in any sense limited to Spain. Sexual liberation was a natural response to the end of the suffocating moral and sexual repression of the Franco era. And as a secondary effect of the pleasure-seeking, as Vázquez Montalbán notes in great detail, came the rise and rise of a new, adventurous, Catalan cuisine.

Other less desirable effects emerged, as a new tourism followed in the footsteps of Genet, seeking the forbidden, the transgressive and the hard drugs that were becoming increasingly available on the late-night Ramblas.

Yet, as Michael Eaude discusses in his *Barcelona*, the structures and restrictions of traditional family life appear to have continued unaffected by this openness. The roles of men and women in the family have largely resisted change: 'In Spain, and Catalonia is no exception, the family comes before everything. The extended rural family has survived the move to the cities, though its shape has become more nuclear. The family, above all, is a buffer for the lack of a welfare state in Spain.' And that has become all the more the case in the recent years of recession, with the dramatic rise in youth unemployment and cutbacks in public services.

It would take a little time before the truth of the end of dictatorship was finally absorbed, the implications of a new democracy acknowledged. In literature, the confrontation with the past would be a first step towards the exploration of the present, and of a discussion of the future.

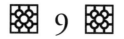

9

THE GOURMET DETECTIVE AND OTHER STORIES

The 'Destape'

In his 1977 article in the *New York Times,* Antony Burgess found the Ramblas breathing the freer air of the *destape*, the sense of a city experiencing the new liberty, or liberation, of the post-Franco age:

> We walk the Ramblas, the wide-avenued district leading to the sea, crammed at noon with strollers, flowers, caged birds and bookstalls. As was to be expected, the new era of liberty has not resulted in a rush of periodicals devoted to free thought, but to a rash of crude publications about sex. Nude covers; frank pictures inside of Spanish teenagers in al fresco fornication, jeans well down for it; articles on how the sexuality of Spanish women compares with that of their democratic sisters. You look in vain for George Orwell's *Homage to Catalonia*; the Barcelonans have forgotten their old British friend and taken to American neutrals like Harold Robbins. In Franco's time, magazine covers showed kittens in ribbons and little girls in Communion frocks; the new popular journalism is franker but ranker. *Sexo* is one new magazine; the latest interviews with nymphomaniacal popsingers and homosexual bullfighters set people panting; the new *Interviu*, with its nippled cover, is in every man's briefcase. The Barcelonans have also discovered, along with democracy, the delights of the soft porn film. I never expected to see the *Pamela* of the great Samuel

Richardson turned into a period eroticon, but there it was, just this summer at the Catalonian seaside resort of Sitges, the women in the audience giggling where their American sisters would yawn. But, in the plazoletas of the Barrio Gótico, a chaster tradition is being upheld at noon – the dance called the sardana. Young men and women in a circle hold their hands high and prance with sedate vigor to music with a Pan pipe.

Francisco Franco died in his bed in November 1975; his designated successor, Admiral Carrero Blanco, had been killed two years earlier in Madrid by a car bomb placed by the Basque group ETA. Franco's act of defiant brutality, just a year before his demise, was the execution of Salvador Puig Antich, a Catalan anarchist, by garrote. Although there was a general expectation of an explosion after 40 years of political and moral repression, the *destape* did not take the expected form of a political frenzy, as Anthony Burgess noted. Instead Barcelona's Ramblas bookstalls – where you could always find a discreetly concealed volume of Marx or Lenin – blossomed with pornography. There was some element of continuity here. The generation of dissident artists and writers of the 1960s occupied the emblematic monastery at Montserrat, the symbolic standard-bearer for Catalan rights, in protest at the Burgos trials of 1970, when leaders of ETA were tried for the murder of a police inspector. Their death sentences were in fact commuted in the face of international protests. Yet in general, Catalan resistance had been individual, agitation for personal and sexual freedoms rather than more broadly political. The struggles of the workers, by contrast, were implacably suppressed.

The occupation of Montserrat generated a new organisation, the Assemblea de Catalunya, formed in 1972, and dedicated to the pursuit of Catalan autonomy. As already mentioned, housing was a central social issue, and residents' associations became active and increasingly militant, filling a vacuum left by the repression of political organisations. The very significant squatters' movement in Barcelona is in many ways the heir to that tradition, though local activism is still very strong. The popular and radical mayor of Barcelona elected in 2015, Ada Colau, came out of the anti-eviction mobilisations, for example. And the semi-clandestine workers' commissions, launched in 1966 from a church in the Sants district, exposed the hollowness of the so-called 'vertical' unions formed by the Franco state. At another level, the wholesale destruction of historical Barcelona to make way for Porcioles's concrete and freeway version of modernity produced a new generation of socially conscious architects.

Montserrat Roig had lamented the absence of protest among her contemporaries – the cultural Bohemianism that took the place of radicalism. For this new generation the resistance to Franco's Spain was personal and sexual. The most style-conscious of them might go to Boccaccio's or to Carrer Tusset off the Paseo de Gracia, promoted as Barcelona's Carnaby Street. But the students and Bohemians of the 1960s sought their alternative world in the streets of the Raval, in the gay bars and transvestite cabarets like the London, near the port. The Raval, after all, represented not simply transgressive Barcelona, but also the rebellious, anarchist city and the tradition of what had once been called the *rosa del foc*, the rose of fire, because of the frequent use of fire as an instrument of protest. Roig's generation rebelled against those writers who had collaborated with, and benefited from, the Franco regime – chief among them Ignacio Agustí, author of *Mariona Rebull*, the Cerberus who guarded Barcelona's official literary circle, the Ateneo. That generation had been silent or complicit in the attempt to kill Catalan culture – with some honourable exceptions, who by and large had had to work beneath the surface or remain silent in the previous decade.

The cultural transition began in the early 1970s. The first independent newspaper to be published since the war (in 1964), *Tele/Xpres*, was a platform for many of the new literary generation. The first daily newspaper in Catalan would have to wait another ten years: *Avui* (*Today*) began publication in 1974, and *Porqué*, an openly anti-Franco news magazine appeared in the same year. One of its editors, Manuel Vázquez Montalbán, would become the most prolific and probably the most successful novelist of Barcelona, which was not only his birthplace but a central actor in his work.

Vázquez Montalbán was born and brought up in the very heart of the Raval, in Carrer En Botella. He barely knew his father, and his mother survived as a seamstress; he spent his childhood and early youth amid the poverty of the Chinese Quarter. In the 1940s, the harshest years of the dictatorship, the population of the Raval were largely single-parent families – the men were in exile, in prison or dead, and prostitution was often the only recourse for the women left behind.

The transgressive thrills of the Barrio Chino that had drawn the Bohemian artists like Genet and Bataille had become more sordid, more down at heel by the 1940s. There was always an element of voyeurism and cruelty in the middle-class tourism into the poor districts. But whereas there is no record of artistic sallies into the Guinardó or Carmelo, the Barrio Chino continued to attract those, like the French writer Andre Pierre de Mandiargues, who travelled in search of the bizarre, the brutal, the encounter between love and death. His novel *La Marge* (*The Margin*) won France's most prestigious literary prize, the Prix Goncourt, in 1967. Its formal elegance and lyrical prose contrasts dramatically with the moral decadence it describes. It is set in the Barrio Chino, where the protagonist, Segismond, spends a kind of lost weekend trawling through the sexual shadows of the city, though he emerges from them at times, to condemn the Columbus column at the bottom of the Rambla as a vulgar phallic symbol. And he is especially exercised by the chickens cooking on the open fire at what was probably the city's most famous restaurant, Los Caracoles, on the Calle Escudellers behind the Plaza Reial.

By the end of the 1970s, the sex industry and the tolerance of it in the years of the *destape* brought a second and more damaging effect – the proliferation of hard drugs, and especially heroin. As the

1980s began, the Barrio Chino and the nearby Plaza Reial became more dangerous places to visit.

The Chronicler of the Raval

Vázquez Montalbán was fortunate enough to be able to go to university, despite his impoverished background. As a student he participated in the demonstrations of the early 1960s and in 1961 was arrested and jailed, but later released under an amnesty occasioned by the death of Pope John XXIII. He then joined the Catalan Communist Party, of which he remained a member despite his pointed criticisms of many of its later actions (for example, in his novel *Murder in the Central Committee* (1981)), and embarked on a journalistic career with the magazine *Triunfo*. His articles were acerbic and gave little quarter in their criticisms of the regime.

His career as a novelist began with *Yo maté a Kennedy* (*I Killed Kennedy*) in 1972. *Tatuaje* (*Tattoo*) introduced his hugely popular detective Pepe Carvalho two years later. Like Montalbán himself, Carvalho was brought up in the Barrio Chino, and his office continues to be there even though, like his author, he has moved into more desirable accommodation in the hills at Vallvidrera. Yet, like Montalbán, Carvalho is irresistibly drawn back to his childhood streets, with their smell of rancid oil, fish and sweat: in Michael Eaude's words, 'Carvalho knows these people and these streets and he wouldn't change them; they make him feel alive. But at night he prefers to flee the defeated city for the steep suburbs from where he can look down on the city as if it were not his own.'

In his study of Vázquez Montalbán's work, *Con el muerto a cuestas: Vázquez Montalbán y Barcelona* (*Carrying the Dead: Vazquez Montalban and Barcelona,* 2012), Eaude describes *Tattoo* as a 'tender portrait of the Raval'. Carvalho is an outsider in the same sense as Philip Marlowe and the Continental Op, the respective

14. *Plaque to Manuel Vázquez Montalbán, creator of Barcelona's gourmet detective Carvalho*

protagonists of the masters of detective fiction, Raymond Chandler and Dashiell Hammett (also a communist). As he explained to Michael Eaude:

> With *Tatuaje* I understood it was possible to write testimonial novels, but in a very different way from socialist or critical realism. The testimony on Spain had to be both playful and distanced; that was the only viable form, given the social conditions in the country. It is a typical neo-capitalist country and the poetics of American noir fiction seemed to me the most appropriate for expressing the living conditions and the organization of this type of society, the

most appropriate for describing its social and political crimes, as opposed to the psychological or naturalist ones – crimes in the modern sense of the word. That's why I wanted to see whether it was possible to realize a cultural fusion within the Spanish realist tradition with American noir fiction. I wanted to develop an ironic chronicle of the transformation of Spain.

Montalbán's success as a novelist grew with his detective protagonist. Carvalho's sympathies and allegiance are with the poor and the marginalised, and deeply hostile to the new rich coming to the surface in the Barcelona of the post-Franco age, the era of 'transition'. A gourmet and a wine connoisseur (again like his progenitor) Carvalho is not averse to pouring away a priceless bottle of wine rather than drink with a wealthy murderer, as he does in *La soledad del manager* (*The Angst-Ridden Executive*, 1977). His early girlfriend, Charo, is a prostitute, his boon companions, Biscuter, a car thief, and Bromide, a disillusioned ex-fascist soldier abandoned by those who recruited him, who now works as a boot-black. Each in their way shares in his marginality.

With Franco's death, there was a general expectation that liberty would serve to unmask those who had been complicit in the dictatorship and benefited from it. Carvalho certainly saw his investigative work in that light. But the transition proved to be compromised from the outset, with the Communist Party and others negotiating away many of their pre-*destape* principles in exchange for a share of power. As the Carvalho novels develop in real time, he himself grows not only older but increasingly cynical and disillusioned. *Los mares del sur* (*Southern Seas*, 1979), for example, has as its main character a capitalist, Stuart Pedrell, who has made his money from gerry-building working-class tower blocks on the city's outskirts. The fictional San Magín is an area of immigrant workers and the poor, the defeated of the Civil War. The speculator yearns to escape, as Paul Gauguin had done, to the exotic South Seas, but he returns a year later and is murdered. It becomes clear that in his crisis of conscience he attempted to compensate for the damage he had done to so many working-class families, but it was too late. Yet in the end, when Carvalho presents his report to the businessman's widow, it is clear that his family and its money will survive largely untouched by his death. By the same token, the communist carworker, Ana Briongos, who also lives in the barrio, has no illusions about the so-called transition or the Moncloa Pact between the Communist Party and the right, including former members of the Franco governments. The Pact of Forgetting, as it was called, simply replaced new elites for old. As Ana says in the novel, 'No one swallowed the Moncloa pact, but we had to defend it with all the good faith we could muster [. . . in the hope] that in the long run it would favour the working class. In short, we spouted what they'd told us to say. Soon everyone saw it was a sell-out, like all the rest.'

Barcelona is more than a background to Carvalho's investigations; it is a living presence in the lives of the characters of almost all the novels, the mirror of their past and their memories at the very moment at which that world disappears to be replaced by another more soulless place: 'The ugly poverty of the Barrio Chino [. . .] had nothing in common with the ugly poverty prefabricated by the prefabricating prefabricators of prefabricated barrios. Poverty is preferable when it is sordid rather than mediocre.'

If there were no drunks in doorways in San Magín as there were in the Raval, it was not a mark of progress: 'The inhabitants of San Magín could not self-destruct until they had paid the debts they had incurred to buy a space for their new life in that new city.' Vázquez Montalbán, like his protagonist, is cynical and angry, but he is also generous to those around him, tender in his dealings with the genuinely vulnerable, and very clear where his allegiances lie.

His next novel, which did not feature Carvalho, is arguably one of the most beautiful novels to have emerged from Barcelona. As with all his books, memory and the impact of the past are central to *El pianista* (*The Pianist*), published in 1986. The setting once again is Barcelona; the time the present of the novel's publication. It begins in the contemporary city, where a group of university friends meet in a night club in the Raval, with transvestite singers and an elderly pianist. We have seen in other novels how the Raval attracted the middle class to what were once the lower depths and now is a kind of simulacrum of its own past, where prostitutes and drag queens play out their earlier roles for visitors. The members of the group had all been students together at a time of rebellion and activism, a time of sexual experiment and public protests, when the imagined future was a post-Franco world of freedom and optimism. But now, ten years on, their lives have taken separate roads, and their past utopian dreams have been replaced by a growing cynicism, which in the case of Schubert, the most vocal of the group, has led to a kind of indifference.

At one point in the Capablanca Club, where they meet the pianist, Albert Rossell, they raise their glasses in a toast.

> 'To the fall of the regime,' Schubert says.
> 'Which regime?'
> 'What difference does it make?'

They were all once members of the 'internal resistance' to Franco. 'At other times they would have come to the area [the Raval] in solidarity with its misery, with the unbreakable ethics of redeemers, but now they tiptoed through it to avoid the razor gangs and the other rabid rats from the system's sewers.'

Their old friend Toni Fisa is now a high-flying academic in the US, Joan and Mercè a wealthy bourgeois couple. 'There is a time to make mistakes,' Joan says, 'and a time to discover why we made them.' In the club, famous for its drag acts, they encounter Javier Solana, a government minister (who would later become NATO's secretary general in real life) and the celebrated composer Luis Doria, who will figure in the novel again. The narrative then follows the elderly pianist home after work, where we see him tending to his sick and bedridden wife.

The second part takes us back to 1946, and to the Raval where Montalbán and Carvalho (and it turns out the pianist too) were born. On the roof of a tenement building the community meets, out of sight of the Civil Guard and the fascist thugs patrolling the street below. As a community they share the hardships of postwar Barcelona. The local hairdresser holds a banquet which consists of olive oil (impossible to find in those times) and bread. The families themselves survive on very little, renting out rooms in their small flats to make ends meet and remembering the dead, the exiled and the imprisoned of their community – of which the Raval had more than its fair share. Young Serra, an amateur boxer, has his dreams of future wealth. Andres has been in prison, but his friend Quintana brings him the banned books that he reads and quotes from at length. The two young women, Magda and Ofelia, boarders in one of the houses, survive from day to day, finding entertainment where they can. On this particular day a new arrival joins them on the terrace, Albert Rosell, the pianist, recently released from jail. He is taciturn at first, until the vibrant banter and human interest of the people on the roof encourage him to tell them something of his life. It is a compelling portrait of a community surviving despite its circumstances in solidarity with one another. At one point the Gypsies in the bar down in the street begin to sing and dance, and the watchers gather to look down and to share a moment of exuberant joy, until the police intervene and disperse the crowd. Later, in a comic progression from roof to roof, the company goes in search of a piano in a neighbouring home. Rosell plays and for a moment the group is overpowered and silenced by the beauty of the music. It is a poignant moment, especially when it emerges that the piano's owner is Teresa, the woman Rosell had previously loved but had lost.

The novel's third part is set in Paris on the eve of the Spanish Civil War, in 1936. Albert has arrived with a scholarship to study at the Conservatoire with a letter of introduction to a rising star in the modern music world – Luis Doria. Doria is a cynical iconoclast, his revolutionary rhetoric mostly bluster, since he refuses to attend the demonstrations or protests that precede the beginning of the Civil War. We know from the earlier sections of the novel that he quickly became the darling of the Franco regime and by the 1980s was a celebrity. In Paris he seeks out the most celebrated writers and artists – Malraux, the composer Milhaud – to bask in their reflected glory. His ambivalence towards a modest and insecure Albert is manipulative and dishonest, since he sabotages the opportunities he promises the young man. Doria's girlfriend, Teresa, is a butt for his cruel jokes and empty promises – and in the end she and Albert will find common cause in their decision to return to Spain, where, we learn later, Albert joins the militia of the POUM. The revolutionaries of the POUM were victims of a purge by the Communist Party during the war, yet Montalbán – who was a Party member – has Albert join the POUM. Asked why, he said that it was because they were the doubly defeated.

The Pianist maintains what is perhaps Montalbán's central and repeated theme – that without a sense of history, and an understanding of the past, we are condemned to repeat its errors endlessly. The cynical opportunist Doria is one expression of that wilful refusal to understand the past; the group in the night club, the very people who might perhaps have ensured that the transition would bring genuine change, have equally given up on their youthful hope. What is left is the modest unassuming humanity of the pianist and the promise of his music.

As Barcelona, and the society as a whole, began to emerge from the suffocating (and violent) conformity of Franco's Spain, the difficulty for writers was twofold. First, those who spoke the truth to power, or described the reality of their own world, were subject to pervasive direct censorship at every level. The dubbing of films was a direct form of censorship, as is often the case under repressive regimes. Many writers – such as Joan Sales or Terenci Moix, among many others – were only allowed to produce truncated versions of their writing under Franco. There was also the indirect censorship that Goytisolo talks about in a society where the enemies of freedom look exactly the same as its defenders – the consequence of all civil wars. The result was self-censorship, or simply silence. And for writers in Barcelona the most important weapon of all was the prohibition of their own language – Catalan.

The first manifestations of resistance – such as the Catalan-language newspaper *Avui*, the magazine *Porqué*, the defiant contestatory public theatre, the new song movement – addressed the limitations on individual freedom and the suppression of collective, and especially trade union, rights. And by the early 1970s, there was an open and active debate about sexual freedom too. A new generation of architects and town planners were openly critical of *porciolisme*, the grandiose building schemes of Porcioles which had served only the speculators at the expense of the residents.

But what remained unspoken was the past, Spain's recent history and its impact on the lives of everyone who lived there. Franco had systematically removed any and every reference to the past as soon as he took control of Barcelona – changing the names of streets and squares, as well as banning the language; indeed, he erased the whole collective experience. The history of Barcelona and Cataluña was not taught in any educational institution, and the books that might have filled the gap were denied publication. Self-censorship and repression had in some sense served to empty the public's memory as well. The inner life of the city, the experience of history and the memory of the past were literature's special and particular contribution. That might explain why so much Catalan writing, notably in recent decades, has been concerned with recovering, or rediscovering, the past. And why much of the first body of work to be published after Franco's death was concerned with the relationship between the present and the past.

Terenci Moix's popular semi-autobiographical novel *El dia que va morir Marilyn* (*The Day that Marilyn Died*) was first published in 1970, although it was severely censored at the time for its sexual explicitness and its criticism of Catholic education. The author returned to the text in 1986, restoring it to its original state as well as rewriting parts of it. In its five sections Moix explores the lives of two characters, Bruno and Jordi, and their families at different historical junctures. It is, of course, an exercise in nostalgia, an exploration of memory. What is especially original about Moix's text, as its title indicates, is the role that cinema in particular and comics and popular culture in general play as markers in the life of each individual. The screen reflects and in a sense interprets the characters' inner landscapes – from 'Cinderella' as a representation of the fantasy world of children to 'Niagara' in which Marilyn's smouldering presence responds to the awakening sexuality of the two boys.

It is at one level a novel about the clash of generations. Bruno's parents, Amelia and Xim Quadreny, tell their story looking back to Barcelona before the war (1928) from the novel's endpoint in 1962. Xim is egotistical and machista. His marriage to the hard-working seamstress Amelia does not restrain his promiscuity nor affect his regular excursions to the prostitutes of the Chinese Quarter. Xim and Amelia's visions of the poor barrio they lived in is idealised, Xim's especially, as a cheerful round of local dances and affairs. When the Civil War ends, they throw in their lot with the new regime, and become rich and successful. The modest Amelia is transformed into an archetypal lady of the Eixample, with all the attitudes and values that an entry into the new bourgeoisie of Franquismo implies. Bruno is a lonely and withdrawn child growing up in a family in which his mother and father's flirtations leave him marginalised and unhappy. His father's affections, such as they are, are invested in the youngest son Carlitus, a sickly boy who dies young. Thus Bruno's sexual awakening, in the repressed moral atmosphere of Barcelona in the 1950s, is sublimated in film – especially in Marilyn Monroe – and in the heroes of the comic books he reads.

Jordi, the son of friends of the family, is his constant companion as they grow into adolescents. But, as he explains in the final section ('1962'), he knew from a very early age that he was homosexual and that his intimacy with Bruno was a friendship shaped by desire. *The Day Marilyn Died* is a narrative of generational conflict and of the very different values that underline the world of parents and children. It is also a portrait of a city about which both boys feel a deep ambivalence as they awaken to their own sexuality and their desires for freedom.

Moix himself shared the fascination with cinema, as many of his books and articles attest. He might be accused, as some critics have, of nostalgia. But, like so many of his contemporaries, in the conditions of a post-Franco Barcelona, looking back is not an evocation of what used to be but a discovery of what was hidden or denied, a kind of secret history without which the future has no basis on which to build. As Moix himself put it in *El dia que murio Marilyn*:

> I am obsessed by forgetting, because I live in Cataluña which is the country of forgetfulness. When I think of the writings of great men it horrifies me to think that their work might be forgotten. But I'm just as horrified by what is forgotten at the level of personal life, because what that means is that we remember only a quarter of our life. Forgetting is a curse of our times and the principal enemy of the human race.

This is more than a general statement about the passing of time; it is a very specific reference to the particular experience of a Cataluña which he insisted should be *mestiza*, embracing all the nations and cultures within it.

If the transition to a post-Franco Barcelona began before the dictator's death, the clean break that many people expected and hoped for did not come immediately. While Franco himself was dead, those who had held power in his name were reluctant to surrender it. On the other side, the organisations that had operated in clandestine conditions under the previous regime were involved in a conflict over their post-Franco role. Nonetheless, it surprised many that the Communist parties of both Spain (PCE) and Cataluña (PSUC) were willing to accept the monarchy that Franco had reconstituted with Juan Carlos as his successor as head of state in exchange for a place at the table of government. It was the price placed upon a negotiated settlement by the still-powerful right. In 1977, a massive demonstration through Barcelona, under the banner of the Assemblea, called for the implementation of the Statute of Catalan Autonomy.

There was certainly public debate about the transformation of Barcelona, especially in the realm of architecture. The grandiose modernity that Porcioles had sponsored did not fulfil any of the promises of earlier eras to humanise Barcelona. On the contrary, the plans in place in 1976 were to involve large-scale demolition of the city's architectural heritage and the continuing construction of massive commercial buildings. The permanent housing crisis had thrown up a network of very active grassroots organisations specifically concerned with housing – and they had plans and projects of their own. The planners of the next phases of Barcelona's development managed to call a halt to the demolition plans and save and restore the architectural heritage which has been the heart of the city's cultural tourism. Would the city still have 20 million annual visitors without Modernisme, the Barri Gòtic or the Raval?

They also gave cohesion to the whole, especially in the decision to avoid wholesale rebuilding and instead to look at each district separately, reforming and rebuilding parts of it while retaining the shape and character of the area as a whole. In a sense, the tension between a construction industry anxious to build hotels and conference centres, and a population looking for a liveable city has been a permanent feature of the post-Franco age, and remains so. And yet, despite the very active grassroots movements that characterise Barcelona, the city administrations have time and again yielded to the temptations of a wealthy construction industry and the pressures of large-scale post-modernist architecture.

Pepe Carvalho was a witness to the changes, or the lack of them, in Barcelona. Montalbán's novels follow the process in real time and Carvalho's ageing is a process at once physical and psychological, the product of disillusionment. His sharp satires of the late 1970s and early 1980s were intended as part of a wider dialogue, a confrontation with the past and the creation of a new and different city.

On 23 February 1981, Spain was reminded that the past had not disappeared. On that day a Civil Guard lieutenant-colonel, Antonio Tejero, occupied the podium of the parliament waving a pistol, and announced a *coup d'état*. The event was televised and seen worldwide. The attempt failed and Tejero was arrested. It may have seemed slightly comic opera, but Tejero had already spent seven months in prison for a previous coup attempt – and his latest effort was, briefly, supported by the tank regiment in Valencia. It was a clear declaration by a military still largely led by appointees of the previous regime, and by its right-wing supporters, of their discontent with the direction Spanish politics was taking. On the following day King Juan Carlos took to the screens to call for calm. But the result of his appearance was to reinforce the 1978 Constitution, which enshrined the consensus of the Moncloa pact. It should be remembered that Juan Carlos, and the monarchy, had been imposed by Franco, who had adopted the young king and made him head of state under the dictator's wing.

In 1982, the Socialist Party of Spain (PSOE) formed the government of the Spanish state for the first time. Three years earlier, its leader, Felipe González, had won an internal battle to remove the word 'Marxist' from the party's constitution. It was an implicit announcement that the party had 'modernised', that it was committed to a continuing parliamentary democracy. In that sense it continued the consensus, the Pact of Forgetting, that was agreed after Franco's death. The curious silence about the Civil War was the pact's most obvious consequence.

Vázquez Montalbán's writings during the early 1980s display a growing disillusionment which becomes a growing anger by the end of the decade – particularly against the corruption that was increasingly exposed during those years, and in which both the Popular Party and the Socialists were implicated. If the successful Olympic bid was represented as a solution to a growing economic crisis by the new city administration, it became clear that whatever new resources they generated would be spent in the luxury and tourist sector, quelling the optimism of the immediate post-Franco period. Montalbán's *El centro delantero fue asesinado al atardecer* (*Offside*, 1989) exposes the financial interests involved in football, just as earlier writings had addressed corruption in the construction industry. By now, everyone was aware that Barcelona Football Club was 'more than just a club' – both as a popular symbol and as a machine for generating a great deal of money.

A Dream of Independence

In Cataluña, the election of the Socialist Party to power in Madrid was very little comfort to those seeking independence. Throughout its 37-year existence, the central government had declared its defence of 'one united Spain', reinforced by its systematic repression of the rights of the Basque or Catalan nations. The Socialist Party, while it recognised (perhaps despite itself) rights to regional autonomy, was defiantly centralist and equally hostile to the idea of those national rights as it was to the idea of a federal Spain. Nonetheless, the 1979 Statute of Catalan Autonomy confirmed the government of the Generalitat with limited powers. From 1980, under the presidencies of Tarradellas and Pujol, the conservative nationalist Convergencia i Unió (CiU – Convergence and Union) party held the majority of seats until 2003 and was returned to power under Artur Mas between 2010 and 2015. Between 2003 and 2010, Cataluña was governed by a coalition including, and led by, the Catalan Socialists of the PSC.

Catalan was now the language of Cataluña, and of Barcelona. The autonomous government promoted learning programmes in schools and for the previous generations, who had spoken it all their lives but who had rarely read or written in Catalan. There was now a Catalan-language press, a boom in Catalan-language publishing and a high-quality Catalan channel, TV3. Significantly, banks and insurance companies began to advertise in Catalan.

Barcelona was certainly changing. The *destape* had proved to be cultural and social, rather than political. The mayoralty of Barcelona passed to the Socialist Party in the shape of Narcis Serra (in 1979) and later Pasqual Maragall, a grandson of the Modernista poet Joan Maragall. Catalan culture, suppressed for so long, became highly visible again. The Giants and Devils, and their ubiquitous fireworks, returned triumphantly to the streets for the feast of La Mercé every September. The city streets filled with people carrying a book and a rose for Sant Jordi every 23 April, St George's Day. The crowds gathered again every 11 September at Santa María del Mar to celebrate La Diada, the commemoration of the siege of Barcelona in 1714 described in Sánchez Peñol's *Victus*. In the Cathedral Square in the Gothic Quarter, the *sardana* was danced every Sunday morning. And at the end of the 1985/6 season, the victory of La Barça, Barcelona Football Club, in the Spanish League, drew all these strands together in a massive public celebration.

The material reality was less unambiguously positive. The industries of Barcelona were slowly dying – both the old and the new. The SEAT factory was up for sale, and between 1968 and 1988 the city lost 70 per cent of its manufacturing jobs. Tourism and construction were the main sources of Barcelona's income. Yet at the same time, 1981 brought a deepening economic crisis in the wake of the oil crisis of the mid-1970s. Against that background the election of a socialist government, just a year after the biggest general strike in the history of the Spanish state, expressed a general aspiration to a welfare state that did not yet exist.

Barcelona was the embodiment of that distorted economic growth. The construction boom, while in the short term it provided generally poorly paid jobs to some sectors of the population, did nothing to address the desperate need for cheap public sector or rental accommodation. For the most part, it directed a greater proportion of resources towards the service sector, linked in one way or another to tourism. But through the 1980s it was still day-trips from the coastal resorts that accounted for most tourism.

For Vázquez Montalbán this new consumerist Barcelona, this gallery of the post-modern, has razed to the ground much of his city. As Bisuter says in *Offside*, 'We'll need to watch out, boss [. . .] they want to demolish half the Barrio Chino, from Perecamps upwards, until it connects with the upper class districts, so that the air can circulate. This is beginning to smell like a cemetery.' As Michael Eaude discusses in his study of Vázquez Montalbán, this is not just the nostalgia of an old man for his childhood streets. We know that those streets were hard and dangerous and life in them was tough. But there was hope there for a better future. Montalbán's anger, especially in the face of the Olympics, was the product of the feeling that hope itself had been taken away. In *El laberinto griego* (*An Olympic Death*, 1991) Carvalho walks through Poble Nou, the early industrial district where now only a few symbolic chimneys remain, and despairs. This was 'a landscape of ruins or foundations, lined by unfinished motorways that connected nothing'.

The final irony is that Montalbán and his wonderful protagonist Carvalho have come to be seen not as implacable critics of political compromise and financial corruption, but as guides to Barcelona and above all to its cuisine, of which Carvalho was a connoisseur.

10

How the World Came to Barcelona

Olympic Dreams and Olympic Realities

In 1936, the International Olympic Committee, having awarded the Games to Barcelona, changed its mind at the last minute and gave them to Hitler's Berlin. We have seen that a different, alternative, Olympics was planned and organised instead. Its opening concert would include the great Pablo Casals as its orchestral director. But the People's Olympiad never took place, nor did Casals play at their opening on 19 July. Instead a military coup on the previous day launched the Spanish Civil War. Six years after the death of Franco, Barcelona presented its candidacy again:

> The Olympic candidature was decided in the summer of 1980, when the city was suffering a cultural crisis, a lack of projects, the misery of a fierce economic crisis, and it was made public in May 1981, just after the attempted coup on 23 February. So we were very aware of the need to generate enthusiasm, to set out some tangible goals that people could see.

The speaker is Narcis Serra, then recently elected socialist mayor of Barcelona. What the 'cultural crisis' meant for him is not made explicit, but it might well have been the disappointment of people's expectations of what the transition from the Franco dictatorship would be like. The carefully managed and gradual transition had left many of the functionaries of the dictator's regime in place. In the previous decade a wide range of neighbourhood organisations had emerged around the city, campaigning on issues of housing, public services, health and education. Many of these, as Vázquez Montalbán and Michael Eaude point out, were far more than protest groups – they designed and developed local projects, from museums to cultural centres. In a crowded city they agitated for a transformation of public spaces, including parks and playgrounds for their children. They often turned to a new generation of architects committed to rescuing the city from the giantism of Porcioles. These groups clearly hoped that a renewed Barcelona would listen and respond. But Serra was quick to clarify that the Catalan Socialist Party was the party in the Barcelona government, and that they were not there to represent the grassroots and community movements. He did, however, put Oriol Bohigas, a leading radical architect, in charge of the city plan.

Barcelona, after all, was a radical city – not only in the pursuit of Catalan independence, but in its revolutionary history and its youthful population, who regularly filled the streets with demonstrations and marches. But the transformation to which Serra and his successor Pasqual Maragall, also a socialist, were committed was imagined on a grand scale. It would launch Barcelona into the modern world as an *international* city; and, given that Madrid would be financing a significant portion of the Olympic dream, it would place less emphasis on its Catalan character. In November 1986, the International Olympic Committee announced from its offices in Lausanne the victory of the Barcelona bid. It fell to Juan Samaranch, ex-minister of sport under Franco, and a cunning operator in a class of his own, to make the declaration.

For the next six years, the Olympics dominated everything, much to the irritation of Vázquez Montalbán. His *Sabotaje Olímpico* (*Olympic Sabotage*, 1993) fulminates against the new Barcelona. The city he had known, and whose streets had been the stage for his fictions, was now at the mercy of the all-night excavators Bisuter had complained about. The great transformation was to occur at the port and along the several miles of beach past the Barceloneta. It would reach back into Poble Nou, a working-class district whose residents had worked at the local factories like La Máquina Terrestre and El Vulcan, and which was now subjected to an accelerated gentrification. Once it had been called the New Icaria, after Etienne Cabet's utopian community. Now it would house a new middle class. Barceloneta would undergo an even more dramatic metamorphosis.

Until the 1980s, Barceloneta remained the poor district it had been throughout its history. Its beaches were neglected and polluted by nearby chemical and textile plants. For Barcelonans, the area was identified with the *chiringuitos*, the beach restaurants under rickety awnings where the paella and the fish were cheap and wonderful and you ate with your feet in the sand. This was still the Barceloneta that had received the largest number of bombs during the Civil War, because it was a place of renowned resistance and radicalism, as indeed it had been before its first demolition in 1714. The Camp La Bota, on the beach, was an execution site used by Franco in the aftermath of the Civil War. None of that past exists today, since the area began its transformation at the hands of the international architects who flocked to the city in the early 1980s and were charged with its Olympic transformation. The beach is there, of course, cleaned up and modernised with elegant restaurants along its boardwalk. Only Rebecca Horn's curiously moving sculptural homage, *The Wounded Shooting Star* (though it is better known as the *Homage to Barceloneta*), remains to commemorate the little restaurants, represented by an awkward pile of windowed boxes sitting on the sand.

Significantly, the Hayward Gallery in London celebrated the new city project with a 'Homage to Barcelona' exhibition in 1985–6. But the Barcelona it referred to was the city that had invited international architectural stars to build its new Olympic waterfront. Perhaps the most emblematic was Frank Gehry, the Los Angeles architect whose

15 Rebecca Horn's
Homage to Barceloneta

headless fish dominates the new beach area and who had already built Bilbao's Guggenheim, and Jean Nouvel, whose Agbar Tower, highly reminiscent of Norman Foster's London Gherkin, defined the new skyline. Gehry's fish is witty, at least, and relevant to the area's history, but the surrounding buildings, like Barceloneta itself, as opposed to the long beach development, remains a poor area. The wider area has become an area of restaurants (not to be confused with the *chiringuitos* of yesteryear), discos and tourist 'attractions' of every kind. The other representative sculpture of the area, the giant prawn at the old port, seems to this writer like a very expensive bad joke. However, the rest of the rebuilding is attractive, the beach is well used, the wooden boardwalk pleasant. But the post-Olympic

Forum development, building around the Olympic Village after the Games ended and intended to define a new culture city, failed.

Eduardo Mendoza, witty and incisive as ever, gave a clear sense of how it felt to live in a Barcelona in full transforming mode. *Sin noticias de Gurb* (*No word from Gurb*) was first published in parts in the newspaper *El Pais,* and then in book form in 1991, the year before the Olympics began. It is by any standards an extraordinarily funny book – which irritated some critics who preferred his earlier, longer, more complex novels. It is, of course, a satire and a brutal critique of the city. The anonymous narrator is an extra-terrestrial who has landed by accident outside Barcelona while searching for his companion, Gurb, without whom he cannot return to his own planet. In searching for him – with the added complication that both of them can take on the appearance of anyone they like – the narrator writes a diary of two weeks in the city. Here is a typical entry:

15.02. I fall into a trench dug by the Barcelona Hydroelectric Company.

15.03. I fall into a trench dug by the Barcelona Water Company

15.04. I fall into a trench dug by the National Telephone Company

15.05. I fall into a trench dug by the Corsica Street residents association.

The diary records the narrator's amazement at the rampant consumerism of the city and the suspicion with which its members treat one another. He gets lost regularly in streets closed for repairs or rebuilding, finds museums closed for remodelling and fails to understand the reasons for the amount of city traffic and the speed at which it circulates.

This is unmistakably Barcelona preparing for the Olympics. For, unlike other cities (like Mexico, for example) which choose to build their athletes' villages on the city outskirts, the municipality of Barcelona looked to the ex-industrial sites and the green-field sites within the city. The most visible consequence is the transformation of Barceloneta and Poble Nou, on the one hand, and the refurbishment of Montjuich and its surrounding area, where many of the events took place, around the Olympic Stadium, on the other.

The early proposals of Bohigas, before he resigned in 1984, made some very exciting changes to the cityscape. His offer of a flat rate to world-famous sculptors to fill and change some urban spaces brought Claus Oldenburg's characteristically witty 'Matches' to the Horta district, the Rebecca Horn to the Barceloneta and (a personal favourite) Botero's plump cat to the Plaza del Raval. As Michael Eaude points out, they are 'anti-monuments', additions to a public space rather than heroic souvenirs. But, as Gurb discovers, the disruption of the city's life, the rising levels of pollution, and the apparent lack of consideration of the impact on the inhabitants, generated a contradictory response from local people. Some left, but many remained and took pleasure in some aspects – like Frank Gehry's fish.

The beneficiaries of the new Barcelona were the multinational companies who built the hotels and the conference centres, the construction enterprises involved in the expansion of the airport at Prat del Llobregat, the Vallvidrera tunnel and the two massive *rondes* (ring roads). The beach at Barceloneta is well used and very popular. Until the Olympic bid was won, there was real investment in public services. Bohigas was an advocate of what was called *esponjament*, a rebuilding programme that did not consist of simply levelling whole areas, as Porcioles had done, but of making internal changes district by district, with knowledge of the specific character of each, mixing social provision and the transformation of public spaces. One result is the Plaza George Orwell, just off the Ramblas beside the Hotel Falcón, which Orwell described in his *Homage to Catalonia*, where the POUM militia had their headquarters, and which today houses the Andreu Nin Foundation. Another emblematic example is the MACBA, the Museum of Contemporary Art in the Plaza dels Angels, in the heart of the Raval. Flooded with light, it sits directly opposite the seventeenth-century chapel after which the square is named. And it has since acquired another accolade, as one of the most famous sites for skateboarders. It is featured in the smartphone game *Skater*.

More symbolic of the changes, perhaps, were the changes in the Raval – the embodiment of both working-class Barcelona and the transgressive underworld with which the area was identified. A new space, the Plaza del Raval, was opened at the heart of the district, with several buildings in the Calle Hospital at one end and Carrer Nou de la Rambla on the other, demolished to open the new square. The Colombian sculptor Botero's Cat sits defiantly at its centre. The population has changed too, in the sense that the new arrivals in the city, who had always gravitated towards its narrow, overcrowded streets, now came from further afield – not just from other areas of Spain but from Asia and Africa too. The poor still found refuge in the Raval, Barceloneta and in the hills beyond. The reality was that the new City of Design and of the Olympics reflected a prosperous middle class consuming global brands and an exploding mass of tourists who came to sample both the old and the new, from Gaudí to Gehry.

The Barcelona Olympics were, it must be said, a stunning spectacle – one that attracted the notice of the world and began to draw increasing numbers of visitors to the city itself, beyond the day-trippers from the Costa Brava. Between 1990 and 2013 the number of overnight stays in the city rose from 1.7 million to 7.6 million. A more recent count of the number of visitors in all categories suggests a figure of 16 million, and rising. (The city's permanent population is stable at around 1.6 million.) Yet many of the city's problems persist. Housing has become a critical matter. The crisis of 2008 and its aftermath caused the construction industry to collapse, both in the tourist sector and in social and affordable housing. The escalating unemployment levels, especially among the young, have exacerbated the phenomenon of younger people living with their parents for much of their lives. Within Barcelona house prices and rents have rocketed, as much accommodation has been adapted for tourists. At the same time, repossessions as a result of the banking crisis took even more housing out of the available stock. Protests about housing and against evictions grew into a powerful movement, one of whose leaders, Ada Colau, is now the popular mayor of the city. Construction has continued, but mainly to expand the hotel and corporate sector, that globalised world of conferences and congresses for whose custom the major cities of the world are endlessly competing. And the rise in tourist numbers, the overwhelming volume of traffic, the pollution of the city continued long after the Olympics had ended with a spectacular Fura del Baus multimedia show.

Private Eyes and Public Spaces

The year 1992 marked a kind of frontier, yet another transition to a future still to be undefined. Colm Tóibín added a final chapter to his *Homage to Barcelona* on the Olympic city.

> As you move around the new Olympic buildings in the city you realise that no new architectural style is on display or has been developed for Barcelona 1992. This city is not the city of a century before, forging its own identity through its buildings [. . .] The style is international now, a bit of Japanese here, a bit of neo-classicism there.

That is almost a definition of post-modernism!

There was a great deal that was new in the post-Olympic city, in fact. But it was not unmistakably Catalan, in the way that the Modernista buildings had been. It is a curious paradox that the reshaping of the city was an affirmation of its place in a modern globalised world. 'But', says Tóibín, 'there was too much of the old city left for the Olympic city to affect it much.' He mentions some of the bars and cafés he had known a decade before, the refurbishment of the buildings of earlier times, the crowded cultural spaces that linked past to present, like the Ramblas. It is also true that much of historical Barcelona has been in a sense restored – or in the case of the city walls, unearthed and exposed, for example immediately behind the Estación de Francia.

What is particular to Cataluña's capital is the residue of the past that is also, and in a way more forcefully, embedded in the language and the culture, and reaffirmed in the impulse to independence from Madrid. The economic argument is that Cataluña provides 19.49 per cent of the central state's tax revenue and receives in return just 14.03 per cent. Much more significant has been the resolute refusal of both major parties in the Madrid parliament to allow Cataluña greater autonomy and control over its own revenues.

Surveys and polls tend to suggest a population split pretty much down the middle on the question of independence. This may have something to do with the large proportion of the population that is of non-Catalan origin. Subsequent events have deepened the suspicion of both Madrid and the conservative nationalists around the CiU Party in the Generalitat.

The global economic crisis of 2008 hit Spain extremely hard, and Barcelona was especially exposed to its impact. The city, like the rest of the Spanish state, experienced dramatically high levels of unemployment, reaching 50 per cent among the young. The housing crisis, already profound, now moved towards the catastrophic. The issue for Barcelona was that the explosion of tourism had exacerbated the problem even more. Construction in the tourist and luxury sector had driven both Catalan and Spanish economies through the previous decade and a half; the financial crisis led immediately to a major crisis in the construction industry as the millions of unfinished apartments along the coast will testify. In Barcelona, however, existing rental flats in the city were increasingly changed into tourist accommodation. Meanwhile many of the young people who had occupied the less salubrious areas of the city were forced to return to their parental home, and the rooms they moved out of were refurbished for visitor use.

On 15 May 2011, millions of young people occupied the central squares of every city in Spain, including Barcelona, in protest at the vast net of corruption that had been exposed by the collapse of 2008, and the failure to address its consequences for the population (as opposed to the rescue packages for the banks). Few leading figures or politicians seemed to escape charges of involvement in corruption, including past president of the Generalitat, Jordi Pujol. The occupation of the squares in 2011, known as 15-M, was extraordinary, a response to austerity, unemployment and the revelations of corruption. The Plaza Catalunya appeared to have found its vocation, under the quizzical gaze of the Telefónica, the Corte Inglés, the Macià Monument and the recently reopened people-watching Zurich Café. The movement was significant not just in its scale but in its methods of organising – through open, democratic public assemblies. Its main slogan, emerging from the movement of the young, was 'No home, no work, no fear'.

Carlos Ruiz Zafón's hugely successful novel, *The Shadow of the Wind*, published in 2001 and in English in 2005, and its sequels, of which there are four, present a Barcelona that is equally part of an international imaginary, more Gothic than Catalan. In the first book, he writes, 'Like all old cities Barcelona is a sum of its ruins. The great glories so many people are proud of – palaces, factories, monuments, the emblems with which we identify – are nothing more than relics of an extinguished civilization.'

But, as we have seen, a great deal of effort has been put into the refurbishment of those ruins, and the rediscovery of their history – the disinterred streets at the Born would be a good example. Of course, there is an element here of what has been called 'the invention of tradition', a phenomenon in no sense restricted to Barcelona. And perhaps that invented past has been sanitised, its contradictions removed or suppressed. At the same time, Barcelona has modernised relentlessly. It is hard to reconcile this 'sum of ruins' with the post-

Olympic city for which and within which the novel was written. It seems quite distant from the dynamic and changing space that Barcelona has been and continues to be. It is hard to resist the feeling that this entertaining novel is set in an imaginary place more akin to Victorian London than Barcelona, part of an imaginary for which history is increasingly entertainment. Perhaps that is its special appeal – that its conventions are recognisable for any contemporary reader with a penchant for Gothic horror or costume drama.

In fact, the cultural atmosphere of post-Olympic Barcelona was shaped by the global movement towards post-modernism, a notion much argued over and in any event open to question. It was, in the first instance, an architectural style characterised by eclecticism, a mixing of conventions, which often parodied what had gone before. In literature it was a refusal to recognise that writers had a duty to represent the world – Realism. The theorists of Post-Modernism, indeed, like Jean Baudrillard, had called into question the very existence of an observable reality as opposed to images or representations of it.

One of the most famous representatives of this current in literature was Roberto Bolaño, a Chilean who lived his latter years in Barcelona, and who saw his 'infrarealism' as an antidote to the Latin American 'magical realism' of García Márquez and others, who had also found Barcelona a welcoming place for new writers in the 1960s and 1970s. But Bolaño set his novels elsewhere. His vision of things produced a new kind of cynicism. If nothing is what it seems, what is left to say about it? If that is the case then we can only know our own inner world and writing can become a rehearsal of how we might go about doing that, or alternatively a way of producing endless possible fictions, or pastiches. Oddly, perhaps, the genre that seemed most amenable to this kind of speculative literature was detective fiction – the *novela negra*.

Pablo Tusset's *Lo mejor que le puede pasar a un cruasan* (*The Best Thing that Can Happen to a Croissant*, 2003) was an immediate success in Europe – where the ubiquity of the croissant in recent times might explain the attraction of the title. Its decidedly anti-heroic protagonist, Pablo 'Baloo' Miralles, is the wayward second son of a wealthy Barcelona family. His older brother, Sebastian, runs the family real estate business while Pablo devotes himself to sleeping, drinking and drug-taking in enormous quantities. He is resistant to exercise and his increasing weight becomes a theme of most conversations with his parents and his friends.

His brother suddenly vanishes, which launches Pablo, reluctantly, on an investigation into his disappearance – though as a thoroughly modern private eye, a large part of the work is done via the internet, about which he is knowledgeable and which he finds fairly easy to negotiate, as opposed to the cars he is occasionally forced to drive. His search takes him on high-speed car chases, into mysterious brothels and into regular contact with the police. In the end, Pablo finds himself sequestered in a kind of post-industrial version of a castle in the heart of Barcelona and yet concealed in the inner heart of its older buildings. Escape from this contemporary version of a Transylvanian castle proves difficult, but it is the only way to save his brother.

There is a curious symmetry between Ruiz Zafón and Tusset's writing; Tusset's novel could be classified as post-industrial Gothic, a parody of its originals yet equally given to endless interconnecting passages, mysterious strangers and false leads. The difference between them, on the other hand, is tone. Tusset's milieu is a distinctly modern Barcelona full of cars driving too fast, pollution and crowds of tourists. His prose is mocking, closer to punk in its irreverence, its social media metalanguage and its fascination with a variety of forms of self-medication. It is in that sense post-modern.

Film and mass culture are key reference points for any twenty-first-century writer; they provide the 'simulacrum', the artificial world in which post-modernism exists. They are also the backdrop to the short stories of Quim Monzó. The tales in the 2007 collection *El millor dels mons* (*The Best of All Possible Worlds*) leave the reader in no doubt that they are ironic. The plots, for the most part, are absurd – but rarely comic – in fact they often border on the sinister, like 'Summer Holidays', in which the husband leaves a stillborn baby in the fridge (it's a long holiday weekend, a frequent problem in the city) and finally delivers it to the hospital in a plastic bag from the Corte Inglés. Or 'La Mama', in which a boy becomes convinced that his mother is a prostitute because someone has called him 'a son of a whore'. He constructs every one of his mother's responses into a narrative that confirms his suspicions. 'My Brother' addresses how a family, and the narrator, avoid acknowledging the sudden death of his brother at the dinner table. These are themes that recur in Monzó's stories – misreadings and misunderstandings, the failure to connect, the elaborate traps that people fall into in their failure to communicate and the fictions we construct. In 'Tot rentant plats' ('All Dishwashing') a couple rent a holiday house in the mountains when an unexpected guest, Xavier, arrives – and stays and stays. He is not welcome but the couple cannot find a way of asking him to leave and he has no understanding of their discomfort. On the other hand, the regular occurrence throughout the text of the phrase '(or not)' suggests that the whole thing may in its turn be imagined. 'I Have Nothing to Wear' consists entirely of a monologue of indecision:

> He changes his shoes and looks at himself in the mirror. He looks OK, but there is something that doesn't quite fit. What if he gave up his idea about a dark shirt and started looking for his red shirt, the one that suits his complexion so well? He takes off his black jacket and gray shirt and puts on his red shirt and, again, the black jacket over that. He looks at himself. No. He takes off his jacket and his shirt. With no time to theorize, he tries on all possible combinations: a beige shirt with the black jacket; a green shirt with the plaid jacket; a yellow T-shirt with the black jacket; the green T-shirt with the gray jacket; a gray T-shirt with the gray jacket; a white T-shirt with the plaid jacket.

The ending, unexpected as it is, underlines the absurdity of the narratives we create around ourselves. Some critics have linked Monzó's writing to the 'fictions' of the Argentine writer Jorge Luis Borges, but he himself (very plausibly) points to the influence of a previous generation of writers of short fiction like Pere Calders and Manuel Pedrolo.

Ruiz Zafón's internationally successful Cemetery of Forgotten Books series, with its settings in the Gothic Quarter, may have some responsibility for the emergence of a new kind of historical novel, like Falcones' *Cathedral of the Sea* and Sánchez Piñol's *Victus*, as well as Chufi Llorens's historical blockbusters – his latest, *La ley de los justos* (*The Law of the Just*) is 1,000 pages long – among others, which look further back towards the medieval city, the War of Succession or, in Llorens's case, to the burgeoning Barcelona of the nineteenth century. The previous generation of writers had focused largely on the city's immediate past through the years of the Franco dictatorship in their memoirs and novels, many of which were semi-autobiographical, as we have seen. There has certainly been a fascination with fictionalised history in recent times – perhaps corresponding to what has been called 'the invention of tradition', a sometimes-sanitised version of the past in response to a new kind of cultural tourism, for which Barcelona caters especially well. But it is in a sense a comfortable, recognisable past.

The same cannot be said of the detective fiction in its various guises that has flowered in Barcelona in the past couple of decades. Until its closure, the excellent bookshop in the Barceloneta run by Paco Camarasa, Negra y Criminal, attracted writers in the genre from all over the world and eventually stimulated a new festival of noir fiction – Barcelona Negra – which encouraged a new generation of writers to emerge and produced a series of annual anthologies under the same name. Camarasa's excellent survey of detective fiction past and present in *Sangre en los estantes* (*Blood in the Veins*, 2017) covers the world but also explores the genre's manifestations within the Spanish state.

Detective fiction was almost wholly absent during the Franco years. That is hardly surprising. Noir fiction travels through a flawed world of corrupt police and politicians, often involved in crime and prostitution. It was highly unlikely that a critical view of the police, on whom the regime rested, would be permitted under Franco. The official view of the city and its moral geography could not admit to the city's inequalities, however visible they were to the naked eye. Francisco González Ledesma's first novel, *Sombras viejas* (*Old Shadows*), published in 1948, won an international novel prize and was then immediately banned. We have seen how Joan Sales's *Uncertain Glory* was heavily censored before its first publication in 1957. And Vázquez Montalbán's first Carvalho novel, *Tatuaje*, was only published in 1975 – a year before the dictator's death.

The very long shadow of Vázquez Montalbán fell across anyone writing in this mould for more than two decades, challenging them with the virtually impossible task of rivalling Pepe Carvalho, his central character. It was interesting that Andrea Camilleri's Sicilian detective Montalbano shared with his Spanish equivalent a passion for food, among other things. And the Italian's name is enough to confirm that the connection was not accidental. But by the time of his death (in 2003 in Bangkok airport), Vázquez Montalbán and his protagonist had become older and more jaded about changing the city.

In many ways Montalbán had foreseen the potential for corruption there, or indeed in any city, following in the steps of Chandler and Hammett; it was already clearly present in *The Angst-Ridden Executive*. But the contrasts between the rich and the poor, which had always characterised Barcelona, were underlined and reinforced as the spectacular new beachside developments and the booming tourist industry diverted resources away from the poor.

The post-Olympic city has become the third most important place for tourists visiting Barcelona from around the world. By the end of 2016, the number of visitors had risen close to 17 million, as the city became a magnet for young revellers, culture seekers, music fans attending one of its many music festivals, and those gathering at conferences along Barceloneta. It also became a popular focus for a new kind of cultural tourism which explored the cities and the interior landscapes of Spain rather than its beaches. A renewed Catalan statute in 2000 affirmed but also limited Catalan autonomy, and a further proposal in 2010 was blocked by the Socialist government.

The promise of a new and more egalitarian city was betrayed, it seemed, by developments directed mainly at a wealthy jet-set, Catalan and international. Montalbán's Raval, where he no longer lived but to which he constantly returned in fact and in fiction, became less glamorous as drug trafficking established itself there. The population of the Raval changed dramatically over the two decades after the Olympics, with a growing Asian and African presence.

Eduardo Mendoza, for example, returned to it fictionally in *La aventura del tocador de señoras* (*The Adventure of the Ladies' Powder Room*, 2017) and *El secreto de la modelo extraviada* (*The Secret of the Missing Model*, 2017). Both books featured a nameless detective who had first appeared in his Gothic novels of the late 1970s and 1980s such as *La cripta embrujada* (*The Enchanted Crypt*, 1978). After a period in a mental hospital, the anonymous anti-hero now reappeared in 2017 as a delivery man for a Chinese restaurant in the Raval. The very visible Chinese presence in the new Barcelona has brought with it the underworld of tongs and secret societies. It is a violent world, populated by an international mafia who increasingly appear in crime fiction, as they did in Tusset's novel and as they do in Andreu Martin's extremely violent *Sociedad negra* (*Black Society*, 2013).

This is no longer the classical detective story as a puzzle to be solved in the manner of Sherlock Holmes or Miss Marple. Ever since Philip Marlowe, Chandler's protagonist, an investigation was not simply a process of discovering the pieces that make up a jigsaw, but a slow unmasking of what lies hidden beneath the surface of the modern city. The more that Barcelona came to resemble London or Los Angeles, the more the model of US noir fiction seemed appropriate. In the novels, the investigation is invariably an occasion for a journey through the city's undergrowth. Petra Delicado, the detective created by Alicia Giménez Bartlett, has very few illusions about the city's rich or its poor. Andreu Martin, from the first post-Montalbán generation, describes a city of violent encounters, both past and present. And he is the first to trawl the world of a Chinese mafia increasingly powerful in the new globalised era.

The Barcelona Negra anthologies, interestingly, are arranged by district – crime, murder, prostitution seemed to have spread beyond the Raval and the Gothic Quarter. Yet the noir model seems to return invariably to the Raval. A novel by Francisco González Ledesma, published in 2007 and the winner of yet another literary prize, can stand as a representative both in content and in tone of the new genre. *Una novela de barrio* (*Where the Poor Live*) has as its central character a police detective born and raised in the Raval, Inspector Méndez. Like Carvalho, he always carries a book or two, but is much less preoccupied with food and life's good things. He eats in local bars and popular restaurants and drinks the harsh liquor of Galicia, *orujo*. But, as he says, he is immune to the diseases that bad food can bring, from having eaten it so often. True to the origins of the genre, Méndez is a policeman viewed with suspicion by his superiors and prone to breaking the laws he is supposed to protect, usually in defence of natural justice rather than the law. He is a policeman in a society where policing is severely constrained by politics and politicians, and where the force is replete with violent and racist people. Méndez, with his big old-fashioned and mercilessly effective Colt 45 ('capable of bringing down a man or a wall', we are told), is also an avenger on behalf of a population of poor and marginal people with whom his sympathy is obvious and open, to the disapproval of his superiors.

In *Una novela de barrio* Méndez has to deal with the consequences of a bank robbery that failed, in which a child was killed and one of the thieves escaped. That was 20 years earlier, in the old Raval, whose inhabitants have grown older and in many cases have left their homes as the developers have moved into the area. But Méndez remembers the district as it was and maintains his contacts with the remnants of the old world. Amores is a radio disc jockey from Andalucia whose ear is attuned to the bush telegraph whose messages circulate on the streets. Méndez hears them too, but the other, newer police, who have no relationship with the street, do not.

The commissioner of police sympathises with Méndez:

I understand, Méndez. Your world is disappearing. The old cafés of Barcelona, where the Republic was declared, and where you watched the evening light decline, have closed one by one, many of them forced to do so by the Ministry of Health. The old Raval isn't what it was any more. They've opened a new avenue through it, they've opened shops seling lactose-free products, and the madams have gone and been replaced by dentists.

Méndez concurs: 'I always speak to people in bars, and the bars speak to me and I find things out. But the good habits are dying out, and people at the bar only talk about football these days. And sometimes not even that!'

As another character puts it:

Look at the thousands and thousands who died defending the Republican cause in Barcelona. What did they get in return? A monarchy – some victory after 40 years of dictatorship. But the monarchy, very sensibly, won't even help them to find where their dead are buried. Oh, it did help them to a second victory – the election of left-wing governments. But the first socialist government understood that there was a market and broke the sacred law of secure employment to defend the market. The second was the slave of the multinationals [. . .] So what did the dead die for, exactly?

It is as if the old Raval, for all its poverty and the dominance of the sex industry, was a place that had some sense of honour and solidarity. Now, however, as a barman friend of Méndez says to him:

> People don't believe in politicians any more, Mr Méndez, but at least they believe in chefs, and that will bring us an era of peace and tranquillity. No chef as far as I know has ever started a civil war [. . .] When people only argue over the best place to eat, the problems will be over. Mind you so will history [. . .] Today cooking is the spirit of the people, Mr Méndez, and we are close to perfection. No one knows the constitution, but people have read the Michelin Guide.

True to its origins, the detective novel unmasks a society that has become cynical and corrupt, and the detective is a lonely and isolated traveller through its mean streets. When asked, Méndez is clear about his vocation: 'I don't believe in the law. But I believe in the victims, and as it happens the law always overlooks them.'

*

On 15 May 2011, as the Plaza Catalunya filled with the young protestors of 15-M, the crime novel came to reflect their vision. In her *Negras tormentas* (*Dark Storms*, 2011), Teresa Solana describes the city as 'a monstrous theme park'. It features her highly atypical inspector in Cataluña's Mossos d'Esquadra police force, Norma Forester, who is a trained anthropologist. Her daughter, Violeta, is an *okupa*, one of Barcelona's many squatters with dreadlocks, and Violeta's father (not Norma's husband) is gay. The murder Norma is called upon to investigate reconnects her with the Civil War in which her father had died as a volunteer in the International Brigades. It is not accidental that the unresolved traumas of the Civil War play a key role here, as they do in much other writing at the time. The issue of historical memory was then, and continues to be, a major issue. While some voices call for the whole issue to be consigned to a buried past, others have taken the opportunity to redefine each side in the conflict as equally responsible for the violence that occurred then. 'For Norma, that cynical attempt to rewrite history to minimise the importance of the crimes committed by the Franco regime, or rather, to silence them in the name of a reconciliation that had never happened, drove her mad.'

In communities all over Cataluña and the Spanish state, that view is shared. The Law of Historical Memory acknowledged their demands at a very late stage; it committed the state to support the search for the unmarked graves of the dead of the Civil War. But the institutions dragged their feet in putting it into effect. It was the efforts of local communities who would not accept forgetting that has carried through its promise in their stead.

What was made very clear at Barcelona's crime fiction festival, Barcelona Negra, in 2014, was that detective fiction was the chosen vehicle of writers concerned with corruption and the widening social gap in the city. Those had always been central features of what was called 'noir' fiction, from Dashiell Hammett and Raymond Chandler to Vázquez Montalbán. Like Montalbán's Carvalho, the private eye is independent of official institutions, cynical but sharp-eyed, and – most fundamentally of all – incorruptible. Two years later, at the 2016 City of Barcelona Literary Awards, Dolors Miquel's savage satire of the Lord's Prayer, 'Padre Nuestro', provoked a storm of protest – proof that even in this radical city religion, feminism and nationalism are still battlegrounds.

In that sense, literature both of and about Barcelona continues to fulfil that role it had so often played in the history we have reviewed here. To speak the truth to power, to 'seek the skull beneath the skin', to discover the past, and to imagine the future.

Barcelona Bookshops

Altair
Gran Via de les Corts Catalans 616
Specialising in travel – books, information and a huge message board for contacts – this is a Mecca for the traveller, literary and otherwise
www.altair.es

La Casa del Libro (3 locations)
Paseo de Gracia 62 (main location)
Rambla Catalunya 37
C.C. La Maquinista, Paseo Potosí 2
Commercial bookskop chain with a number of branches
www.casadellibro.com

La Central del Raval
Calle Elisabets 6
Well-established in the heart of the Raval, close to the MACBA Art Centre. Housed in an attractive eighteenth-century building, it has a range of books in several languages and a pleasant café to read them in
www.lacentral.com

Documenta
Calle Pau Claris 144
Specialising in art and literature, with a wide range of graphic novels too. It was located for many years in the Barri Gòtic but is now in the Eixample close to the Paseo de Gracia metro station
www.documenta-bcn.com

Fatbottom
Carrer de la Lluna 10
Specialising in the world of graphic novels and graphic works more generally, located in the heart of the Raval
www.fatbottombooks.com

FNAC

Plaza de Catalunya 4

Originally a French radical bookshop, since expanded into a series of major cultural department stores that offer new books, music, electronics, newspapers, coffee and practically everything else. There are several branches in Barcelona but the major one is right in the centre at Plaza Catalauña

www.fnac.com

Hibernian

Carrer Montseny 17

As the name suggests, this has a very large collection of books in English, as well as Spanish, Catalan and French. Located in the fashionable Gracia district

www.hibernianbooks.com

Libreria Etcètera

Calle Llull 203

A fine bookshop with a wide ranging stock, it has been a favourite meeting place for book lovers for 40 years, with frequent talks and readings. It is a little out of the centre in the increasingly fashionable Poble Nou district

www.etc-llibres.com

Libreria Re-Read

Gran via de las Corts Catalans 564

A fairly new national chain, it carries both new and second-hand books – and even a book exchange – at reasonable prices

www.re-read.com

El Lokal

Carrer de la Cera 1

At the heart of the counter-culture of the Raval with newspapers, pamphlets and books on radical politics, movements and feminism, with regular events, readings and presentations – the place to discover what is happening on the counter-cultural scene

www.ellokal.org

Select Bibliography

Where the book details include the name of the translator, I have quoted from that edition. Where no translator is mentioned, I have translated the extracts in the text from Spanish or Catalan.

The editions listed here are those consulted and quoted from; the dates given in the text are usually that of first publication.

Writers referred to in the Guide

Agustí, I., *Mariona Rebull*, Barcelona, Planeta, 1973.

Aribau, C., 'La patria', 1833.

Aub, M., *Diario de Djelfa*, Madrid, Visor, 2015.

—— *Field of Honour*, trans. Gerald Martin, London, Verso, 2009.

Blasco Ibáñez, V., *Mare nostrum*, Madrid, Catedra, 2014.

Burgess, A., 'Homage to Barcelona', *New York Times* , 4 December 1977.

Cabet, E., *Travels in Icaria*, trans. Leslie J. Roberts, Syracuse, NY, Syracuse University Press, 2003.

Calders, P., *The Virgin of the Railway and Other Stories*, trans. Amanda Bath, Oxford, Aris and Phillips, 1991.

—— *Croniques de la veritat oculta*, Barcelona, Eds 62, 2001.

Camarasa, P., *Sangre en los estantes*, Madrid, Austral, 2017.

Candel, F., *Han matado a un hombre, han roto un paisaje*, Barcelona, G. P., 1972.

—— *Donde la ciudad cambia su nombre*, Barcelona, G. P., 1973.

—— *Los otros catalanes, veinte años después*, Barcelona, Plaza y Janes 1986.

Cervantes, M., *Don Quixote*, trans. John Rutherford, London, Penguin, 2003.

Falcones, I., *Cathedral of the Sea*, trans. Nick Caistor, London, Black Swan, 2009.

García, B., *Am buns altres ulls Ed Roca*, Barcelona, Ed Roca, 2016.

García Lorca, F., *Doña Rosita the Spinster*, in *Lorca Plays, Vol. 1*, trans. Gwynne Edwards, London, Methuen, 1989.

Genet, J., *A Thief's Journal*, New York, Grove Press, 1994.

—— *Our Lady of the Flowers*, trans. Bernard Frechtman, London, Faber and Faber, 2015.

Giménez Bartlett, A., *Death Rites*, trans. Jonathan Dunn, London, Europa, 2008.

González Ledesma, F., *Sombras viejas*, Barcelona, Destino, 2007.

—— *Una novela de barrio*, Barcelona, Rba, 2007.

Goytisolo, J. A., *Forbidden Territory and Realms of Strife*, trans. Peter Bush, London, Verso, 2003.

—— *Marks of Identity*, trans. Gregory Rabassa, London, Serpent's Tail, 2003.

—— *Palabras para Julia*, Barcelona, Lumen, 2015.

Guimera, A., *Marta of the Lowlands: Terra Baixa*, trans. Jose Echegaray and Wallace Gillpatrick, Whitefish, MT, Kessinger, 2010.

Hemingway, E., *For Whom the Bell Tolls*, London, Arrow, 1994.

Hughes, L. *Collected Poems*, London, Vintage Classics, 1995.

Laforet, C., *Nada*, trans. Edith Grossman, London, Vintage, 2008.

Langdon-Davies, J., *Behind the Spanish Barricades*, London, Secker and Warburg, 1936.

Lee, L., *A Moment of War*, London, Penguin, 1992.

—— *As I Walked Out One Midsummer Morning*, London, Penguin, 2014.

Llorens, C., *La ley de los justos*, London, Vintage Español, 2015.

MacNeice, L., *Autumn Journal*, London, Faber and Faber, 2013.

Malraux, A., *Days of Hope*, London, Penguin, 1970.

Maragall, J., *Obra poética, versión bilingüe*, Madrid, Clasicos Castalia, 2000.

Marsé, J., *Ronda de Guinardó*, Barcelona, Delbolsillo, 1984.

—— *Si te dicen que cai*, Barcelona, Delbolsillo, 2011.

—— *Ultimas tardes con Teresa*, Barcelona, Delbolsillo, 2015.

—— *La oscura historia de la prima Montse*, Barcelona, Delbolsillo, 2016.

Martin, A., *Sociedad negra*, Barcelona, Rba libros, 2013.

Mendoza, E., *The City of Marvels*, trans. Bernard Molloy, London, Harper, 1990.

—— *The Truth About the Savolta Case*, trans. Nick Caistor, London, Harper 1993.

—— *No Word from Gurb*, trans. Nick Caistor, London, Telegram Books, 2007.

—— *The Mystery of the Enchanted Crypt*, trans. Nick Caistor, London, Telegram Books, 2008.

—— *El secreto de la modelo extraviada*, Barcelona, Planeta, 2017.

—— *La aventura del tocador de señoras*, Barcelona, Planeta, 2017.

Mendoza, E. and C. Mendoza, *Barcelona modernista*, Barcelona, Seix Barral, 2003.

Moix, T., *El dia que murio Marilyn*, Madrid, Austral, 1970.

Moliner, S., *The Whispering City*, trans. Mara Faye Letham, London, Abacus, 2016.

Monzo, Q., *El mejor de los mundos*, Barcelona, Anagrama, 2007.

Mora, V., *Los plátanos de Barcelona*, Barcelona, Buyblos, 2007.

Oller, N., *La febre d'or*, Barcelona, Labutxaca, 2012.

Orwell, G., *Homage to Catalonia*, London, Penguin, 2000.

Padura Fuentes, L., *The Man who Loved Dogs*, trans. Anna Kushner, London, Bitter Lemon, 2014.

Pedrolo, M., *Trajecte final*, Barcelona, Eds 62, 2009.

—— *Typescript of the Second Origin*, trans. Sara Martin, Middletown, CT, Wesleyan University Press, 2018.

Pieyre de Mandiargues, A., *The Margin*, trans. R. Howard, Calder, 1970.

Pla, J., *Un senyor de Barcelona*, Barcelona, Eds Destino, 1989.

Quart, P., *Els millors poemes*, Barcelona, Proa-Coumna, 1998.

Rodoreda, M., *In Diamond Square*, trans. Peter Bush, London, Virago, 2014.

Roig, M., *Noche y niebla: los catalanes en los campos Nazis*, Barcelona, Ed Peninsula, 1978.

—— *Tiempo de cerezas*, Barcelona, Ed Peninsula, 1978.

Ruisinol, S., *L'auca del senyor Esteve*, Barcelona, Selecta, 1977.

Ruiz Zafón, C., *The Shadow of the Wind*, London, Weidenfeld and Nicolson, 2005.

Sagarra, J. M. de, *Private Life*, trans. Mary Ann Newman, Brooklyn, Archipelago, 2015.

Sales, J., *Uncertain Glory*, trans. Peter Bush, London, MacLehose, 2016.

Salvat-Papasseit, J., *Obra completa. Poesia i prosa*, Barcelona, Galàxia Gutenberg , 2006.

Sánchez Piñol, A., *Victus: The Fall of Barcelona*, trans. Daniel Hahn, London, Harper, 2014.

Sand, G., *A Winter in Mallorca*, trans. Robert Graves, London, Cassell, 1956.

Segui, S., *Escuela de rebeldía*, Barcelona, Ed Periferica, 2013.

Serge, V., *Birth of Our Power*, trans. Richard Greeman, New York, PM Press, 2015.

—— *Midnight in the Century*, trans. Richard Greeman, New York, New York Review of Books, 2015.

Solana, T., *Negras tormentas*, Barcelona, Rba, 2011.

Swinburne, H., *Travels Through Spain in 1775 and 1776*, London, 1776.

Tóibín, C., *Homage to Barcelona*, London, Picador, 2010.

—— *The South*, London, Picador, 2015.

Tusset, P., *The Best Thing that Can Happen to a Croissant*, trans. Kristina Cordero, Edinburgh, Canongate, 2005.

Vázquez Montalbán, M., *El centro delantero fue asesinado al atardecer*, Barcelona, Planeta, 1989.

—— *The Pianist*, trans. E. Plaiste, London, Quartet, 1989.

—— *Barcelonas*, trans. Andrew Robinson, London, Verso, 1992.

—— *El laberinto griego*, Barcelona, Planeta, 1998.

—— *Offside*, trans. Ed Emery, London, Serpent's Tail, 2001.

—— *An Olympic Death*, trans. Ed Emery, London, Serpent's Tail, 2008.

—— *The Angst-Ridden Executive*, trans. Ed Emery, Brooklyn, Melville House, 2012.

—— *Murder in the Central Committee*, trans. Patrick Camiller, Brooklyn, Melville House, 2012.

—— *Southern Seas*, trans. Patrick Camiller, Brooklyn, Melville House, 2012.

—— *Tattoo*, trans. Nick Caistor., Brooklyn, Melville House, 2013

Vázquez Montalbán, M. and P. Vivas, *Barcelona*, Barcelona, Triangle Postals, 2006.

Verdaguer, J., *Selected Poems*, trans. Ronald Puppo, Chicago, University of Chicago Press, 2007.

Verne, J., *20,000 Leagues Under the Sea*, trans. David Stuart Davies, London, Wordsworth Classics, 1992.

Wilder, T., *The Bridge of San Luis Rey*, London, Penguin, 2000.

Writing About Barcelona

Beevor, A., *The Battle for Spain: The Spanish Civil War, 1936–39*, London, Weidenfeld and Nicolson, 2007.

Borkenau, F., *The Spanish Cockpit*, London, Pluto, 1986.

Calpena, E., *Barcelona: una biografía*, Barcelona, Destino, 2015.

Canet, E., *Bombardement de Barcelona*, Paris, Hachette, 1843.

Cunningham, V., *The Penguin Book of Spanish Civil War Verse*, London, Penguin, 1980.

—— *Spanish Front: Writers on the Civil War*, Oxford, Oxford University Press, 1986.

Ealham, C., *Anarchism and the City: Revolution and Counter-Revolution in Barcelona 1898–1937*, Chico, CA, AK Press, 2010.

Eaude, M., *Barcelona: The City that Reinvented Itself*, Nottingham, Five Leaves, 2008.

—— *Con el muerto a cuestas: Vázquez Montalban y Barcelona*, Barcelona, Ed Alreves, 2012.

Fraser, R., *Blood of Spain*, London, Penguin, 1994.

Fuster, J., *Literatura catalana contemporania*, Mallorca, Ed Curial, 1975.

Hughes, R., *Barcelona*, London, Panther, 2001.

Lloyd, N., *Forgotten Places: Barcelona and the Spanish Civil War*, Barcelona, Create Space, 2015.

Moorhead, C., *Gellhorn: A Twentieth-Century Life*, New York, Holt, 2004.

Moreta, M., *Historias de Barcelona*, Barcelona, Moreta, 1971.

Sanchez Suarez, A. (ed.), *Barcelona 1888–1929: modernidad, ambicion y conflictos de una ciudad sonada*, Madrid, Alianza Editorial, 1994.

Sartre, J. P., *Saint Genet*, trans., Bernard Frechtman, Minneapolis, University of Minnesota Press, 2012.

Sobreques i Callico, J., *Historia de Barcelona*, Barcelona, Mondadori, 2008.

Tremlett, G., *Ghosts of Spain: Travels Through a Country's Hidden Past*, London, Faber and Faber, 2012.

Vallejo, M. and D. Escamilla, *La Barcelona del Vent*, Barcelona, L'Arca, 2008.

Villar, P., *Historia y leyenda del Barrio Chino*, Barcelona, Ed La Campana, 1996.

Index

Titles that appear in Spanish first are untranslated; translated titles appear with the title in English first, then the Spanish title in brackets.